BY
GRACE
ALONE

BY GRACE ALONE

FINDING FREEDOM AND PURGING LEGALISM FROM YOUR LIFE

DEREK PRINCE

www.derekprince.com

Published by DPM-UK
Kingsfield, Hadrian Way,
Baldock, SG7 6AN, UK
www.dpmuk.org

Library of Congress Cataloging-in-Publication Data is on file at the Library of Congress, Washington, DC.

ISBN: 978-1-908594-97-6
Product Code: B114

Unless otherwise indicated, Scripture quotations are from the New King James Version. Copyright © 1982 by Thomas Nelson, Inc. Used by permission. All rights reserved.

Scripture quotations identified NASB are from the New American Standard Bible®, copyright © 1960, 1962, 1963, 1968, 1971, 1972, 1973, 1975, 1977, 1995 by The Lockman Foundation. Used by permission.

Scripture quotations identified NIV are from the Holy Bible, New International Version®. NIV®. Copyright © 1973, 1978, 1984, 2011 by Biblica, Inc. Used by permission of Zondervan. All rights reserved worldwide. www.zondervan.com

Scripture quotations identified KJV are from the King James Version of the Bible.

This book was compiled from the extensive archives of Derek Prince's unpublished materials and edited by the Derek Prince Ministries editorial team.

Cover design by Dual Identity

Derek Prince Ministries
www.derekprince.com

Contents

Introduction

"I believe legalism is the greatest single problem of the Christian Church."

"The ultimate purpose of this book is for you to discover what does and does not matter in your Christian walk. I believe for each of us, this is a matter of critical importance."

"Confusion on this issue is the root of most of our problems."

These dramatic, sweeping statements by Derek Prince are the keynotes of the book you are holding in your hands, *By Grace Alone: Finding Freedom and Purging Legalism from Your Life.*

Having identified the major problem of legalism facing every one of us, Derek proceeds to help you eliminate it from your life, leading you into a revolutionary understanding of the grace of God.

It is important that you recognize from the start that the focus of *By Grace Alone* is not just on the problem of legalism. Far from just uncovering the negative, Derek moves quickly to a positive, comprehensive treatment of the grace of God that could very well change forever your understanding of the power of this principle in your relationship with Jesus Christ.

It is very fortunate for us that as Derek unpacks this important subject, he does so much more than simply point out the problem. Chapter by chapter in *By Grace Alone*, he moves us steadily through a process of identifying and defining legalism, its origin, and its deadly impact upon the life of every believer, as well as upon the modern-day Church. Moving quickly from an astute analysis of the problem, Derek makes the turn to a refreshing, liberating treatment of the most wonderful antidote to legalism: the grace of God.

The second statement quoted above sets the tone for what Derek Prince's teaching in *By Grace Alone* is intended to accomplish. It answers basic questions for each of us like these:

- What really matters most in my walk with Jesus Christ?
- Have I been focusing on the wrong principles and activities?
- Have I been wasting my time in fruitless pursuits?

- Have I relegated myself to a life of rules and regulations?
- What impact can God's grace have upon my daily experience?

Compiled from a series of spoken messages entitled "Which Way to Righteousness: Law or Grace?" the crystal-clear instruction Derek lays out on the subject of law vs. grace will settle questions that have plagued Christians for centuries. But *By Grace Alone* is not a theological treatise aimed at seminary students. *It is for you.*

Have you entered the ring with religious legalism and lost the fight? Do you want clear and practical teaching that will establish true north for your life? Do you want to embark upon a new understanding of God's grace that will lead you to life and liberation?

If your answer to each of those questions is yes, we encourage you right now to grip this book tightly in your hands, run—don't walk—to the nearest comfortable reading area you can find and dive into this rich teaching by Derek Prince.

Just a few more words of encouragement. Prepare yourself to feed sumptuously on some of the most life-transforming practical teaching you may have ever found. Prepare your heart to sing for joy as you free yourself from the chains and vestiges of religious legalism. Prepare your mind and spirit to enter into newfound life and liberation as you absorb and apply practical impacts of the grace of God upon your life.

Our hope and prayer is that by the time you finish *By Grace Alone*, you will have arrived at new heights and landmarks in your spiritual journey—and that you will be inspired to climb even farther and higher.

Derek Prince, a rather experienced spiritual climber himself, would have wanted it that way.

—The International Publishing Team
of Derek Prince Ministries

1

The Two Ways
to Righteousness

Do you have problems that seem to have no logical solutions? Do you struggle unsuccessfully to make headway in your walk of faith? Do you wonder sometimes just what is right and what is wrong in God's eyes?

What I am going to tell you may surprise you, but I feel quite certain that there is an answer for you, and it has to do with one of the most important teachings of the Bible. Over the years I have become convinced that Christians fail to live the kind of lives God wants us to live, or enjoy the salvation that He has provided, because we are unclear in our understanding of this vital teaching.

What is it? It is the relationship between *law* and *grace*. Many of the problems Christians experience relate directly to their understanding—or misunderstanding—of these two paths to righteousness. Yet, consider the emphasis the Bible places upon it. One entire epistle (or letter) of Paul—the epistle to the Galatians—is devoted to this subject. In its six chapters the phrase *the law* occurs 28 times. Apart from Galatians there are at least 27 other chapters in the New Testament that touch on the relationship between law and grace. In other words, *law vs. grace* is one of the major themes of New Testament teaching.

Yet very few believers understand this. They try one path, then the other, then perhaps try to straddle the two, having no clear picture of the distinctions.

Let's begin our study with some basic definitions. Then we will look briefly at the opening and closing pages of the Bible, and see how law and grace span the millennia. But this is not simply an exercise in Bible education. This theme of *law vs. grace* has indescribable impact on our lives, particularly as we turn to face the end of the ages.

What you are about to read in this book, properly understood, has the potential to change your life for the good from this point onward. In simple terms, it can enable you to find true freedom and to purge the deadly power of legalism from your life.

What Is Law?

In our study, the word *law* refers to *religious* law. Our teaching does not apply to secular or civil law, which is a means of preserving social order. Secular or civil law is a necessity;

it is ordained of God. All Christians should be in submission to the law of the land and other forms of civil or secular law that may apply to them. Instead, we will be studying law viewed *as a means of achieving righteousness with God.*

As an introductory text, look at Romans 10:4, where Paul makes a profound and far-reaching statement: "For Christ is the end of the law for righteousness to everyone who believes."

I marvel at the accuracy of Scripture when I consider that these various books were not philosophical treatises, but letters written under pressure in strange circumstances in somebody's home or in a jail. It seems obvious that the Holy Spirit was guiding every word that was written—in spite of difficult or trying conditions.

In this passage Paul is saying that the moment a person believes in Jesus Christ, in the way that experience is defined in the New Testament, that is the end of law for that person as a means of righteousness. That event is *not* the end of religious law as a part of the Word of God, for law will endure forever. Nor is it the end of law as a record of Israel's history. It *is*, however, the end of law as a means to achieve righteousness with God. There are no exceptions for Jew or Gentile; it is to "everyone who believes."

Remember, the moment you exercise faith for salvation in Jesus Christ, that ends law as a means of righteousness. This simple statement by itself, when carried to its logical conclusion, would make the most far-reaching changes in almost all sections of the Christian church if it were understood and applied.

The Law of Moses

When we use the phrase *the Law* in these studies, we will use it in the same way as the New Testament does: to mean specifically *the Law of Moses*. It is most important to understand this. *The Law* (used with the definite article *the*) throughout the New Testament always means "the Law of Moses."

In Ephesians 2:15 Paul uses this phrase: "the law of commandments contained in ordinances." The *commandments* are the direct requirements of prohibitions—the Ten Commandments: Thou shalt not commit adultery, Thou shalt not kill, Thou shalt not steal, etc. The *ordinances* are the way of living that works out the commandments; certain deeds you had to do and certain procedures you had to follow, such as restoring lost property or bringing an appropriate offering to the house of God.

The entire Law, then, is summed up in the phrase "the law of commandments contained in ordinances."

You might think, "But I'm a Gentile. I was not brought up under the Law of Moses, so these studies will not concern me." Yet in fact, they do, because of what Paul says in Romans 2. In this passage Paul is explaining the function of the Law. He says that even though Gentiles, for the most part, were never brought under the Law of Moses, yet in a certain sense they have become a law to themselves.

> For when Gentiles, who do not have the law [the Law of Moses], by nature do the things in the law, these, although not having the law, are a law to themselves, who show the work of the law written in their hearts, their conscience also

bearing witness, and between themselves their thoughts accusing or else excusing them.

Romans 2:14–15

Notice, it is not the Law that is written in the hearts of the Gentiles. It is the *work* of the Law. In other words, there is in the heart of a Gentile something that operates in the same way the Law of Moses does for a Jew. What does the Law do for the Jew? The Law presses home the question of personal responsibility and personal guilt. Thus, inside a Gentile there is something like a law court. In this court the thoughts of the Gentiles are either accusing them or else excusing them, and their consciences sit as judges.

The "Thought" Court

By way of example, I have observed while traveling in many nations that, for many different peoples, lying is regarded as a sin; however, this is not true of all people. Some people tolerate lying; for some it is a question of whom you lie to. For a Muslim it is wrong to lie to a fellow Muslim. But under certain circumstances, it may be all right to lie to somebody who is not a Muslim. Even so, most cultures have certain rules about lying.

Consider a Gentile whose code of ethics says it is wrong to lie. For some reason he tells a lie. When he lies, the "law court" inside him comes into operation. One thought says, *You just told a lie.*

Then a second thought replies, *Well, it wasn't really a lie. It was just a different way of expressing the truth.*

15

To which the first thought responds, *No, you told a lie. You knew it wasn't true.* This Gentile's conscience, meanwhile, is the judge. We see inside such a person, therefore, the *operation* of the Law. It is not the Law of Moses itself, but the functioning of the Law inside the mind and heart of that person. Thus, the *work* of the Law will do for a Gentile what the Law of Moses was designed to do for a Jew.

Paul makes this point so his readers will understand that his teaching about the Law does not apply merely to people of Jewish background. It applies to all people because all have some kind of moral or legal code operating inside them. I do not believe there is a single exception to this principle. We can say in some way or another, therefore, whether strongly and effectively or weakly and ineffectively, that we each know what it is as a Gentile to be a law to ourselves. Something works inside each of us that functions like a law. If we look back over our lives we can probably remember many incidents when this law court went into operation inside our hearts and minds. We were trying to excuse ourselves, and yet at the same time we were our own accusers. Our consciences were there to give the verdict. This is *the work of the Law* written in our hearts.

A Variety of Laws

If we look at Christendom (the whole spectrum of professing Christians), we find various forms of special religious law. These laws are not part of the Law of Moses, but are regarded as solemn and necessary by the people in that particular group. Whether Protestant, Catholic, Orthodox, Pentecostal or non-denominational, each group has a set of rules or principles by which the members are expected to live.

Consider the followers of the Roman Catholic Church, which, at least until recently, lived under a rigid religious law. That set of laws was not the Law of Moses, nor was it found in the New Testament—and yet it was regarded by them as essential for achieving righteousness. At one time, for instance, it was considered sinful for a Catholic to eat meat on Friday or not to attend mass on Sunday. It is still considered sinful for a Catholic to marry a non-Catholic. None of these rules is in the New Testament; neither are they part of the Law of Moses. But they are very real religious laws for the people who are affected by them. And the effect of these laws is the same for Catholics as the Law of Moses is for Jews in the way it operates in their hearts.

In the Holiness and the Pentecostal tradition, groups with which I am familiar, there are numerous rules or laws that are regarded as extremely important for righteousness. You must not, for example, consume alcohol, you must not smoke, and you must not go to movies. None of these rules is stated anywhere in the New Testament. (It has always surprised me that the people living under the rule about going to a movie in a theater see nothing wrong in viewing the same movie on television inside their homes, because that activity is not prohibited by their law.) In some sections of the Holiness movement women are not permitted to wear makeup or jewelry, and certain lengths are specified for their dresses. If their children attend youth camps, in some cases mixed swimming is not permitted. All sorts of other regulations are spelled out for what kinds of clothing are proper.

If you have never been in a group like these, you may find their laws strange and amusing. For those brought up in those groups, however, these are serious issues, and people feel condemned and guilty if they violate such laws.

It reminds me of a Jewish friend who was brought up in a fairly strict Orthodox Jewish home. He told me that the first time he ate ham he really expected to die; he was genuinely not sure he would survive the experience. Once he got over the first shock, however, he found it rather enjoyable! I have known Christians who believed that if they were in the movie theater when Jesus returned, they would miss the rapture. But once they understood what really mattered to God, they found they could enjoy movies.

I trust you understand from these examples that we are not talking about something that is remote. Religious laws apply in some measure to every person reading this book. I would guess that at least 90 percent of professing Christians are not clear as to what really matters in regard to righteousness in God's eyes. The ultimate purpose of this book is for you to discover what does and does not matter in your Christian walk. I believe for each of us, this is a matter of critical importance.

What Is Grace?

Now let's consider the definition of *grace*. To try to define *grace* is almost presumptuous, but the definition I will use is this: "that which is freely given by God and received by faith, without being earned or deserved."

This definition of grace gives us two important facts. The first and most important fact is that *we cannot earn it, and we can never deserve it.* Anything that we can earn or deserve is not grace. The second fact is that *grace is normally received by faith.* Ephesians 2:8–9 makes this clear: "For by grace you have been saved through faith, and that not of yourselves; it is the gift of God, not of works, lest anyone should boast."

Someone might think of himself as very spiritual and say, "Well, I was saved by grace, but, after all, at least I had the faith to receive the grace." According to this Scripture, however, God could reply, "Yes, but don't forget, I gave you the faith. You didn't even have that of yourself."

Grace has nothing to boast about. I believe that one of the hardest things for a person to receive is the free grace of God, because we always tend to think we have to do just a little to earn it or deserve it. You may prefer to believe there was some special reason why God should have chosen you, but that is not what the Bible teaches.

Two Ways of Righteousness

In all human history and in all the revelation of Scripture there are only two possible ways to achieve righteousness. Anybody who seeks to achieve righteousness is going to follow one or the other. Furthermore, each way excludes the other. If you go one way, you cannot go the other way—you cannot mix one with the other. One way is by *the works of law* and the other is by *grace through faith.*

I do not know how to press this point sufficiently, but confusion on this issue is *the root of most of our problems.* People want to mix a little law and a little grace, but God does not allow it. If something is of law, then it is not of grace. And, if something is of grace, then it is not of law.

Consider these verses from Scripture. First of all, John 1:17 says: "For the law [the Law of Moses] was given through Moses, but grace and truth came through Jesus Christ." Please notice the word *but* in this passage. How did the Law come? By Moses. How did grace and truth come? By Jesus Christ. They are absolutely distinct.

Then, Romans 6:14 says: "For sin shall not have dominion over you, for you are not under law but under grace." Notice the delineating words in the latter part of the verse: *not . . . but*: "*Not* under law *but* under grace." If you are under grace, you are not under law. If you are under law, you are not under grace. You cannot be in both conditions.

Also, please take note of this amazing statement: Sin shall not have dominion over you. Why? Because you are not under the Law, but under grace. And the converse is also true: As long as you *are* under the Law, sin *will have* dominion over you.

Throughout this book, I will emphasize this point continually because it is the root of so many problems. Most believers hold the conviction that grace is really the correct way for a Christian to live. But if they find grace too difficult, then they reason that it is all right to live by law. Law may not work as well, but basically they expect to get the same result more or less.

As I understand the revelation of Scripture, this is completely wrong. Grace and law are not two alternative ways of doing the same things. They are two opposites that produce directly and diametrically opposite results.

In Romans 10:5–6, Paul is writing about law and grace:

> Moses writes about the righteousness which is of the law, "The man who does those things shall live by them." But the righteousness of faith speaks in this way, "Do not say in your heart, 'Who will ascend into heaven?'" (that is, to bring Christ down from above).

The Law is clear. If you want to be made righteous by the Law, then you must do everything the Law says all the time. If you can accomplish that feat, then you do not need grace. But, if you cannot be justified by the Law, then you must accept grace or not be justified at all.

The Law says, "This is what you have to do and to keep doing all the time." Grace says, "Someone else has done it for you."

Two Kinds of Religion

I believe that there are only two possible kinds of religion in the world. There never have been more than two and there never will be more than two. One is a religion of *law and works*; the other is a religion of *faith and grace*. I also

21

believe, by divine design, that these two types of religion are presented to us at the very threshold of human history. One is the religion of Cain, which is the religion of law and works; the other is the religion of Abel, which is the religion of faith and grace.

The presentation of these two religions is the first recorded incident of human history after the Fall. To me, it has become increasingly more significant that these religions are presented to us at the onset of redemptive history. Let's read the account of how this concept was introduced:

> Now Adam knew Eve his wife, and she conceived and bore Cain, and said, "I have acquired a man from the LORD" [*Cain* means "gotten, acquired, achieved"]. Then she bore again, this time his brother Abel [*Abel* in Hebrew is *habal*, and it means "vanity or frustration"]. Now Abel was a keeper of sheep, but Cain was a tiller of the ground. And in the process of time it came to pass that Cain brought an offering of the fruit of the ground to the LORD. Abel also brought of the firstborn of his flock and of their fat. And the LORD respected Abel and his offering, but He did not respect Cain and his offering.
>
> Genesis 4:1–5

This passage indicates that the Lord bore testimony that He had accepted Abel's offering, but He withheld the testimony of acceptance from the offering of Cain. Furthermore, it was obviously done in such a way that the Lord's preference was known to all concerned. However it happened, God's testimony was not something invisible. Most commentators believe that a supernatural fire fell upon Abel's sacrifice and consumed it. We cannot prove this, but we do know for sure that there was a supernatural testimony of favor attributed to Abel's offering that was withheld from Cain's offering. And this made Cain furious. Nothing upsets religious people more than to tell them that their religion does not work.

At the end of verse 5, we read, "And Cain was very angry, and his countenance fell." A different look came on Cain's face. I believe that the sanctimonious religious mask slipped and something else appeared that had lain hidden underneath.

> So the LORD said to Cain, "Why are you angry? And why has your countenance fallen? If you do well, will you not be accepted? And if you do not do well, sin lies at the door. And its desire is for you, but you should rule over it." Now Cain talked with Abel his brother; and it came to pass, when they were in the field, that Cain rose up against Abel his brother and killed him.
>
> verses 6–8

Bear in mind, religion was the source of the first murder ever committed.

The writer of Hebrews gives us further information about their offerings: "By faith Abel offered to God a more excellent sacrifice than Cain, through which he obtained witness that he was righteous, God testifying of his gifts; and through it he being dead still speaks" (Hebrews 11:4). Notice what the writer of Hebrews emphasizes: It was *by faith* that Abel brought his offering, and Abel's offering received supernatural testimony from God.

In the table below you will see seven points in which Abel's religion differs from Cain's religion. As we compare these two religions, I want to emphasize once again that there are really only two religions in the world. Every human religion that has ever been practiced falls into one or the other of these two categories.

The Two Kinds of Religions
(see Genesis 4:1–8)

Abel's Religion	Cain's Religion
1. Involved faith (see Hebrews 11:4)	Did not involve faith
2. Received God's word (see Romans 10:3)	Refused God's word (compare Romans 10:3)
3. Offered propitiation—a slain lamb (see Romans 3:25)	Offered man's own works—the product of earth, which God had cursed (see Genesis 3:17)
4. Was accepted by God (see Genesis 4:4)	Was rejected by God (see Genesis 4:5)
5. Received supernatural testimony (see Hebrews 11:4)	Received no supernatural testimony (see Genesis 4:5)
6. Produced a martyr (see Genesis 4:8; Hebrews 11:4)	Produced a murderer (see Genesis 4:8)
7. Will produce the Bride (see Revelation 19:7–8)	Will produce the Harlot (see Revelation 17:1–6; 18:1–4, 23–24)

Let's take a look at each of these seven points.

The Matter of Faith

Beginning with point one, the writer of Hebrews notes that *Abel offered by faith*. The implication of this statement about Cain seems to be clear: Cain did not offer by faith. He just brought an offering because it was something he decided to do. Romans 10:17 tells us that faith comes by hearing the Word of God. So, if Abel offered by faith, it means that he had some type of a word from God in which he placed his faith. Revelation had been granted to the human race concerning the type of offering that God would accept, and Abel acted on that revelation in faith.

Regarding God's Word

This brings us to point two: *Abel received God's word, and Cain refused God's word.* Cain evidently did not accept the revelation that was made available to the human race. In connection with this thought, we need to consider Paul's words to the Romans concerning Israel in his own time: "For they [Israel] being ignorant of God's righteousness, and seeking to establish their own righteousness, have not submitted to the righteousness of God" (Romans 10:3).

If we seek through our own works to establish our own righteousness, we are refusing to submit to the righteousness of God, which is by faith. There is a rebellion within us against the Word of God, which was also in Cain. Cain was a rebel. He refused to accept the revelation of God's word.

Propitiation for Sin

This leads to the third point: Abel offered a sacrifice that, by its death and shed blood, acknowledged the need for propitiation for his sin. We find the word *propitiation* used in Romans 3:25. Propitiation describes a sacrifice that cancels sin and satisfies the wrath due from God toward sin. In this passage Paul is speaking about the death of Jesus Christ, and we see in Christ's death the fulfillment in God's purpose—a purpose that Abel's slain lamb merely foreshadowed. Paul writes: "Whom God set forth as a propitiation by His blood, through faith, to demonstrate His righteousness, because in His forbearance God had passed over the sins that were previously committed."

Through faith in His blood, we acknowledge that Jesus Christ is the propitiation for sins we have committed. The sacrifice of Abel's lamb was just a foretype of the death of Jesus, the Lamb of God on the cross. Abel offered a propitiation and, in so doing, he acknowledged that there was a sin that needed to be propitiated. Cain did not offer a propitiation. There was no sacrifice, no death and no shed blood. He brought the works of his own hands—the fruit of the earth. Bear in mind that, according to Genesis 3:17, Adam's sin brought a divine curse upon the earth:

> Then to Adam He said, "Because you have heeded the voice of your wife, and have eaten from the tree of which I commanded you, saying, 'You shall not eat of it': Cursed is the ground for your sake."

From this point onward, the ground was cursed. In a sense, Cain offered an affront to God, because he offered Him the fruit of something that God had declared to be cursed. When we offer God our own religious works, therefore, we are offering God the outcome of something that God declared already to be unacceptable. Why? Because He has already declared that we are rebels, and He cannot accept a rebel's deeds.

An Acceptable Sacrifice

Here is the fourth point: *Abel's sacrifice was accepted by God; Cain's sacrifice was rejected by God.* Please note, there is no middle ground. Your relationship to God is either one of acceptance or it is one of rejection. There is no neutrality.

God's Response

The fifth point is important: *God sovereignly bore supernatural testimony to His acceptance of Abel's sacrifice.* By the same token, God withheld supernatural testimony from Cain's offering. I am convinced from the study of Scripture that wherever God by revelation requires us to believe and take certain steps, He will always give supernatural attestation to His own revelation.

If God says, "In faith I require you to do this," then when we do it, we have a right to expect that God will supernaturally attest to His approval of what we do. As I have studied religion throughout the Bible, I find that every time a person in faith accepted divine revelation and acted upon it, he received a supernatural testimony from God. Furthermore, I believe there is something wrong with a religion that does not have a supernatural attestation.

This was just the point at issue that made Cain so angry. His brother received a supernatural testimony, and he did not!

I find that this continues to make people angry. This is the very reason why speaking in tongues, working of miracles and other supernatural manifestations of the Spirit are attacked by religious people today. They are irritated because they are doing a lot of work and not getting the supernatural attestation from God. The apostles had supernatural attestations, I have had them, and I believe every Bible-believing Christian should have supernatural attestations of his or her faith. If we do not have them, something is missing.

Martyrdom

Points six and seven bring us to the "nitty-gritty"—the final results of the two religions. Point six is this: *Abel's religion produced a martyr.* What did Cain's religion produce? *A murderer.* I would venture to say that religions will ultimately produce either martyrs or murderers.

The Final Outcome

Our final point looks forward to the close of the age. Scripture indicates that in all of Christendom only two groups will exist. They will not be Catholic and Protestant, nor Presbyterian and Baptist. God assigns different names for them: One group will be called the Bride, the other group will be called the Harlot. Everybody who survives to the end of the age will be in one or the other. *Abel's religion will produce the Bride. Cain's religion will produce the Harlot.*

Consistently throughout human history, the enemies and persecutors of Abel's religion have been the followers of Cain's religion. Which religion did the Pharisees and the religious leaders in the time of Jesus follow? They were following the religion of Cain, the religion of works and law. And, as a result, they did the works of their father who was a murderer. Jesus tells them plainly, "You are of your father the devil. . . . He was a murderer from the beginning" (John 8:44). The final result was that they murdered the One who preached grace and faith.

The Dramatic Conclusion

I mentioned above in the final point that the story of the religions of Cain and Abel reaches its conclusion at the end of the ages. I want to explore this a little further.

In the book of Revelation, two women are predominant: One is a Bride, the other is a Harlot. As we noted, one is the product of Abel's religion; the other one is the product of Cain's religion. In Revelation 17 and 18 we read the description of the Harlot, an elaborate false religious system.

> Then one of the seven angels who had the seven bowls came and talked with me, saying to me, "Come, I will show you the judgment of the great harlot who sits on many waters, with whom the kings of the earth committed fornication, and the inhabitants of the earth were made drunk with the wine of her fornication."
>
> So he carried me away in the Spirit into the wilderness. And I saw a woman sitting on a scarlet beast which was full of names of blasphemy, having seven heads and ten horns. The woman was arrayed in purple and scarlet, and adorned

29

with gold and precious stones and pearls, having in her hand a golden cup full of abominations and the filthiness of her fornication. And on her forehead a name was written:

MYSTERY,

BABYLON THE GREAT,

THE MOTHER OF HARLOTS AND OF THE ABOMINATIONS OF THE

EARTH.

I saw the woman, drunk with the blood of the saints and with the blood of the martyrs of Jesus. And when I saw her, I marveled with great amazement.

Revelation 17:1–6

This religious system, from the line of Cain, is filled with murder. It martyrs the followers of Jesus. We then read further in Revelation:

After these things I saw another angel coming down from heaven, having great authority, and the earth was illuminated with his glory. And he cried mightily with a loud voice, saying, "Babylon the great is fallen, is fallen, and has become a dwelling place of demons, a prison for every foul spirit, and a cage for every unclean and hated bird! For all the nations have drunk of the wine of the wrath of her fornication, the kings of the earth have committed fornication with her, and the merchants of the earth have become rich through the abundance of her luxury." And I heard another voice from heaven saying, "Come out of her, my people, lest you share in her sins, and lest you receive of her plagues."

Revelation 18:1–4

Note that this religious system is filled with evil, and the people of God are warned to separate themselves from it.

> "The light of a lamp shall not shine in you anymore, and the voice of bridegroom and bride shall not be heard in you anymore. For your merchants were the great men of the earth, for by your sorcery all the nations were deceived. And in her was found the blood of prophets and saints, and of all who were slain on the earth."
>
> Revelation 18:23–24

The secret power in this system is the satanic and the supernatural: sorcery. False religions are not just different ways of looking at truth. Their origin is satanic. This passage also indicates that every murder originates from false religions.

In the discussion of law and grace, we are not dealing with something unimportant and trifling. This is a topic of major significance—not only for us as individuals, but for our understanding of world history and of current events.

We said at the beginning of this chapter that the term *the Law* as it is used in the New Testament refers to the Law of Moses. Since the Law of Moses is such an important theme in the New Testament, we will consider it more closely in the next chapter.

2

Seven Facts about the Law of Moses

Because the New Testament places so much emphasis on rightly relating to the Law, and because so many Christians misunderstand its position in our lives, I want to devote this chapter to seven facts about the Law of Moses.

Fact #1: The Law Was Given through Moses

In chapter 1 we considered John 1:17: "For the law was given through Moses, but grace and truth came through Jesus Christ." Look also at Romans 5:13–14: "For until the law sin was in the world, but sin is not imputed when there is no law. Nevertheless death reigned from Adam to Moses." The time period from Adam to Moses was the period *until the Law*. During this time the world had no God-given system of religious law. Mankind was ruled by conscience. But when Moses came, the Law was then given through him. It was a single act at a single point in human history.

Fact #2: The Law Is a Closed System

The Law of Moses is a complete, perfect system to which nothing can be added and from which nothing must be taken away.

The Law was given initially in Exodus, but about forty years later, just before Israel was due to enter the Promised Land, Moses recapitulated the Law to them, found in the book of Deuteronomy. *Deuteronomy* by its title means "the recapitulation of the law." Moses solemnly warns the people: "You shall not add to the word which I command you, nor take from it, that you may keep the commandments of the LORD your God which I command you" (Deuteronomy 4:2).

God gave it exactly the way He intended it to be. There were no slips, no errors, no omissions. Moses confirms this in Deuteronomy: "Whatever I command you, be careful to observe it; you shall not add to it nor take away from it" (Deuteronomy 12:32).

According to God's command, the Law is completely unchangeable. Jesus, in His Sermon on the Mount, reaffirms this:

"Do not think that I came to destroy the Law or the Prophets. I did not come to destroy but to fulfill. For assuredly, I say to you, till heaven and earth pass away, one jot or one tittle will by no means pass from the law till all is fulfilled."

Matthew 5:17–18

No language could say more clearly that the Law is not to be meddled with. A "jot" is the smallest letter in the Hebrew alphabet, about the size of an English comma. A "tittle" is a little mark on the top of some letters that distinguishes them from other letters, and it is smaller than a comma. Thus, Jesus says in so many words, "So exact and so perfect is the Law as given through Moses that not one little letter or even one part of a letter is ever to be removed from it." Paul writes as well that there is nothing wrong with the Law: "The law is holy, and the commandment holy and just and good" (Romans 7:12).

Fact #3: The Law Means All or Nothing

If we wish to achieve righteousness by keeping the Law, it must be all or nothing. There is no in-between.

This is precisely the point where the human mind likes to play little games with God. The Lord is clear, however, that either you keep the whole Law all the time or you do not bother with it at all, because the Law is of no avail unless you keep it perfectly.

Paul tells us: "As many as are of the works of the law are under the curse; for it is written, 'Cursed is everyone who does not continue in all things which are written in the book of the law, to do them'" (Galatians 3:10).

This statement should give everybody reason to pause. Anyone who is seeking to be made righteous by the works of the Law is under a curse. Once you come under the Law, you have no more options. You must continue at all times to do all the commands written there. If at any point you fail, you are under a curse. Not even one omission or exception is tolerated.

James reiterates this:

> For whoever shall keep the whole law, and yet stumble in one point, he is guilty of all. For He who said, "Do not commit adultery," also said, "Do not murder." Now if you do not commit adultery, but you do murder, you have become a transgressor of the law.
>
> James 2:10–11

Even if you keep 99.9 percent of the law but fail in one-tenth of 1 percent, you are a lawbreaker. It is *all* or it is *nothing*.

Fact #4: Christ Fulfilled the Law

In Matthew 5:17, we read Jesus' words: "Do not think that I came to abolish the Law or the Prophets; I did not come to abolish but to fulfill" (NASB). Scripture indicates that Christ fulfilled the Law of Moses in three distinct ways.

First, *Jesus kept the Law perfectly*. He is the only person under the Law who ever kept the entire law without breaking one point at any time. In John 8:46, we read that Jesus said

36

to the religious leaders of His day, "Which of you convicts Me of sin?" Of course, none of them had even one point they could put an accusing finger on. We can believe that if Jesus ever violated the Law in any detail, they would have known all about it. He kept the Law perfectly.

Second, *Jesus fulfilled the Law by fulfilling all its prophecies.* Everything the Law prophesied about the Messiah, Jesus fulfilled. Luke records the words Jesus spoke to His disciples after His resurrection:

> "Ought not the Christ to have suffered these things and to enter into His glory?" And beginning at Moses and all the Prophets, He expounded to them in all the Scriptures the things concerning Himself.
>
> Luke 24:26–27

The name *Moses* here represents the *Torah,* the first five books of the Old Testament including the Law, which are attributed to the authorship of Moses. (Christians generally refer to these five books as the *Pentateuch,* which comes from two Greek words meaning "five" and, roughly, "case"— a reference to the cases that held the scrolls. The writings *about* the Law and traditions are the *Talmud.*) Everything the Law and the Old Testament books of the prophets predicted about the Messiah was fulfilled in Jesus. He fulfilled "all the Scriptures."

Third, *Jesus fulfilled the Law by paying its final penalty on our behalf.* This is perhaps the most important way in which Jesus fulfilled the Law. In Romans 6:7 we read, "For he who has died has been freed from sin." This is the New

King James translation, but it is not a literal translation of the Greek. The text is best translated: "He that is dead is justified from sin." In other words, the last thing the Law can do to you is put you to death. It does not matter if you have committed fifteen capital offenses, the Law can put you to death only once. And, when it has put you to death, that is the end. It can do nothing more to you, because when you are dead you are no longer under the Law. The Law is a life sentence. Jesus, however, died for all who were under the Law. He suffered the death penalty on our behalf.

In Romans 7:4 Paul writes, "Therefore, my brethren, you also have become dead to the law through the body of Christ." Paul is saying that when Christ died, He died as my representative; He paid my penalty. Christ died to the Law—and I died to the Law through His death. Because I am in Christ, therefore, the Law has nothing to say to me. I am outside its territory, its jurisdiction, finally and forever. There is nothing more to worry about because it is finished.

Paul makes the same point in Galatians 2:19–20 where he applies this truth to himself: "For I through the law died to the law that I might live to God. I have been crucified with Christ." In other words, Paul is saying: "The Law sentenced me to death and I died. The Law and I have nothing more to do with one another. Death has separated us, because Christ's death was my death. When He died on the cross, I died in Him. That was the end of the Law for me."

Christ fulfilled the Law, then, in three ways: one, by keeping it perfectly; two, by fulfilling all its prophecies; and, three, by paying the final penalty.

38

Fact #5: Christ Broke Down the Wall of Separation

We return to Romans 10:4: "For Christ is the end of the law for righteousness to everyone who believes." If you "believe," then Christ is the end of the Law for you—whether you are Jew or Gentile. As a result, a wall of division is broken down between all who believe. In Ephesians 2:11–22, Paul addresses the difference between Jew and Gentile—a Jew being one who was close to God and a Gentile being one who was far from God.

> For He Himself [Jesus] is our peace, who has made both [Jew and Gentile] one, and has broken down the middle wall of separation, having abolished in His flesh the enmity, that is, the law of commandments contained in ordinances, so as to create in Himself one new man from the two, thus making peace.
>
> verses 14–15

When Paul talks about the "wall of separation," he is referring to a certain wall in the Temple in Jerusalem beyond which no Gentile was allowed to pass. There was, in fact, a very real wall of division between Jew and Gentile in Paul's day. He says, however, that Jesus has broken down that wall of division separating Jew and Gentile because He abolished in His flesh the Law of commandments contained in ordinances. Thus, by His death, Jesus has put an end not only to the Law, but also to the enmity between Jew and Gentile.

If we are honest, we must admit there is enmity between Jew and Gentile. It exists primarily because the Law has separated Israel from all other peoples. It is a fascinating fact that when you are under a religious law, it puts you at enmity with those who are not under the same law. Why are the Baptists at enmity with the Episcopalians? It is because of their religious laws. Why are the Catholics at enmity with the Protestants? It is because of their religious laws. Religious law produces enmity.

The trouble with the Church is that we as Christians have re-erected the middle wall of partition. Now, however, it is not solely between Jew and Gentile. We now use other labels, such as Baptist, Catholic, Methodist, charismatic or Holiness. Every time we establish religious law, we reap enmity.

Jesus abolished that enmity by His death because He put an end to religious law "so as to create in Himself one new man from the two, thus making peace." There is nothing new about a Gentile or about a Jew. But what is new is that we are all in Christ as one new man.

When Christ put an end to the Law, He removed not only the enmity between believers, but also the enmity between us and God. In Colossians 2:14–16, Paul writes about the result of the death of Christ on the cross:

[God has] wiped out the handwriting of requirements that was against us, which was contrary to us. And He has taken it out of the way, having nailed it to the cross. Having disarmed principalities and powers, He made a public spectacle of them, triumphing over them in it. So let no one judge you in food or in drink, or regarding a festival or a new moon or sabbaths.

In our hymns, we sing that Jesus nailed our sins to the cross. That is not, however, what the Bible teaches. Paul wrote that Jesus nailed *the Law* to the cross. The Law stood between God and us. It had to be taken out of the way before we could be accepted by God. Notice that Paul said "the *handwriting* of requirements." Why *handwriting*? Because God *wrote* the Ten Commandments with His own finger (see Exodus 31:18), and my estimate is that only God can wipe out what God has written.

In Colossians 2:16, we see the practical application. The New King James starts with *So*, but the Greek says, *Therefore*. Whenever you see a *therefore*, you need to find out what it is *there for*. This *therefore* is so placed because of the preceding two verses that state that God has blotted out the handwriting of ordinances. "So let no one judge you in food or in drink, or regarding a festival or a new moon or sabbaths."

The Ten Commandments are included in that which has been "wiped out." This is confirmed by what we read earlier in Ephesians 2:15: Christ "abolished . . . the law of commandments contained in ordinances." If I believed I were under the Commandments of the Old Testament, I would, for instance, have no logical alternative but to be a Seventh Day Adventist and worship on Saturday in order to keep the Sabbath day. No one can ever convince me that Sunday is the Sabbath. The Christian Sunday is different in its origin, in its nature and in the way it is observed.

I am glad that Paul put in that *therefore*. He wrote plainly that you should not let anyone judge you in what you eat, in what you drink, your religious observances, the celebrating of the new moon or keeping the Sabbath days. Thus, if a Seventh Day Adventist comes to me and wants me to feel guilty because I am not observing the Sabbath, I would have to reply, "God told me not to let you judge me in respect of the Sabbath. Because Christ is the end of the Law for us, the Commandments of the Old Testament can no longer speak to us in regard to righteousness."

Fact #6: Christians Are Not under the Law

Paul states this plainly: "Sin shall not have dominion over you, for you are not under law but under grace" (Romans 6:14). He explains it more completely in Romans 7:4:

> Therefore, my brethren, you also have become dead to the law through the body of Christ, that you may be married to another—to Him who was raised from the dead, that we should bear fruit to God.

Here Paul has been addressing the problem that was particular to the Jews. Every Jew who is confronted with the claims of Jesus Christ and who is prompted to accept them is always tormented by the suggestion that he or she is going to be a traitor to his or her own people. Jewish people believe that they are betraying something sacred.

Paul expresses the Jews' freedom from their obligation to the Law with an illustration from marriage. If a woman is married to a man, and she wants to marry another man while the first man lives, to do so would make her an adulteress.

But if her first husband has died, she is set free from the law of that husband, and she is free to marry the other man.

Paul is saying that Israel was married to the Law, and as long as the Law lived, if Israel were to turn to anyone else, she would rightly be labeled adulterous. But what Israel had to learn is that the first husband has died, and she is now free to be married to Christ, the resurrected Messiah, without being adulterous and without committing spiritual treason. In verse 6, therefore, Paul concludes: "But now we have been delivered from the law, having died to what we were held by, so that we should serve in the newness of the Spirit and not in the oldness of the letter."

We have been delivered from the Law in order that we might live "in the newness of the Spirit." When we are led by the Spirit, we are not under the Law: "For as many as are led by the Spirit of God, these are sons of God" (Romans 8:14). How do you live as a son of God? You are led regularly by the Spirit of God. That is the mark of His children.

This is restated in Galatians 5:18: "If you are led by the Spirit, you are not under the law." The only way you can live as a child of God is by being led by the Spirit. The moment you go back under the Law, you are not living as a child of God any longer and you have lost your inheritance.

Fact #7: Christians Are Warned against Going Back

Finally, consider the solemn warning of Paul about the Law in Galatians 3:1–4. The power of these Scriptures overwhelms me, and I often marvel at how long it took me to see what Paul is saying here. The only thing that surprises me more is that most Christians *still* have not seen the urgency of Paul's warning, which begins right in verse 1: "O foolish Galatians! Who has bewitched you that you should not obey the truth, before whose eyes Jesus Christ was clearly portrayed among you as crucified?"

Is it possible for Spirit-baptized Christians to be bewitched? It must be, or Paul would not have made this statement. Then he asks, "Haven't you seen Jesus on the cross paying the final penalty, putting an end to the law?"

Paul then asks a very telling question: "This only I want to learn from you: Did you receive the Spirit by the works of the law, or by the hearing of faith?" (verse 2). He asks them if they had to be circumcised before they received the baptism with the Holy Spirit, or if they received it by faith after listening to the preacher. Then he adds: "Are you so foolish? Having begun in the Spirit, are you now being made perfect by the flesh? Have you suffered so many things in vain—if indeed it was in vain?" (verses 3–4).

This is a very solemn thought. If you go back under the Law, all the rest is vain. As you read Galatians, you see that Paul is deeply concerned. He speaks of them as "my little children, for whom I labor in birth again until Christ is formed in you" (Galatians 4:19).

It is an amazing fact about the Galatians that there were no moral problems in the Galatian church. In the Corinthian church, on the other hand, there was a man cohabiting with his father's wife, there was drunkenness at the Lord's Table, and there were deep divisions in the church. Yet when Paul started the letter to the Corinthians, he took time to thank God for the grace of God that was bestowed upon them.

When he wrote to the Galatians, however, who had no moral problems but were going back under the Law, he did not take even one moment to thank God for them. He said, "I marvel that you are turning away so soon from Him who called you in the grace of Christ, to a different gospel" (Galatians 1:6). He was much more upset over the Galatians with their legalism than he was over the Corinthians with their immorality and their drunkenness.

In concluding his letter to the Galatians, Paul writes: "Stand fast therefore in the liberty by which Christ has made us free, and do not be entangled again with a yoke of bondage" (Galatians 5:1).

The "yoke of bondage" to which Paul refers is the Law. We talk about bondage to drugs, alcohol and other forms of addiction—all of which is of valid concern. But the bondage that so concerned Paul was the bondage to the Law.

> Indeed I, Paul [Paul puts his personal authority into what he is about to say], say to you that if you become circumcised [as a way of observing the Law], Christ will profit you nothing. And I testify again to every man who becomes circumcised that he is a debtor to keep the whole law.
>
> verses 2–3

You cannot choose one little part of the Law and say, "I'm going to do that" but leave out the rest. It is all or nothing. And once you attempt to be justified by the Law, Christ is of no more avail to you. This is exactly what he says in verse 4: "You have become estranged from Christ, you who attempt to be justified by law; you have fallen from grace."

Looking again at Romans 8, we see that Christians are presented with two alternatives: "As many as are led by the Spirit of God [first alternative], these are sons of God. For you did not receive the spirit of bondage again to fear [second alternative]" (verses 14–15).

This is a vivid description of legalism. The word *bondage* is a rather mild word, and we may not be disturbed by it. The literal translation is "slavery." When you go back under the Law, you come under the spirit of slavery to fear. The Law says, "Do this! And if you don't do it, you are a transgressor!" Or, "Do that! And if you don't do it, you will die!"

The spirit of slavery motivates us by fear. If we are honest, looking back over the past centuries, the majority of Christians have been under the spirit of bondage to fear. Their religion has been motivated by fear of doing the wrong thing, being found guilty and going to hell. That spirit is not from God! This is such a critical issue that I want to come back to it in a subsequent chapter.

So far in this book, we have considered two ways of seeking to obtain righteousness. One way is by *the works of law* and the other is by *grace through faith*.

If we cannot achieve true righteousness with God through the Law, then for what purpose was the Law given? Is it of any use for us today? This is the subject of our next chapter.

3

Why the Law?

In chapter 1, we saw that there are two—and only two—paths to achieving righteousness with God. One is by keeping the works of the Law—and keeping them perfectly all of the time. The other is by grace through faith. We cannot have it both ways; we must choose one or the other.

By the death of Jesus on the cross, however, Christians have been freed from the requirement to keep the Law as a means of righteousness. In addition, we are solemnly warned against going back under the Law.

We might wonder: If the Law is impossible for us to keep, and if trying and subsequently failing to keep the Law would put us under a curse, for what purpose did God give the Law in the first place? In this chapter we will study the six purposes for which the Law was given. Then, in the next chapter, we will consider the effects that the Law produces in the lives of those who try to keep it.

1. Not As a Means to Righteousness

It is important for us to begin with the reason for which the Law was *not* given. God never expected anybody to achieve righteousness by keeping the Law. Paul states this clearly: "Therefore by the deeds of the law [the keeping of the Law] no flesh will be justified in His sight" (Romans 3:20). Other than Jesus, who kept the Law perfectly, no other human being will ever achieve righteousness by keeping the Law.

Two passages in Galatians make this clear: "A man is not justified by the works of the law" (2:16), and "that no one is justified by the law in the sight of God is evident" (3:11). The Bible is clear: No one, apart from Jesus, ever will be justified or achieve righteousness in the sight of God by keeping the Law. If the Law was not given to make us righteous, then why was it given?

2. To Reveal Sin

The Law was given as God's diagnostic means to reveal sin. When you go to a doctor today and tell him, "Doctor, I feel kind of strange inside and I get dizzy spells," he does not reach up to the shelf, pull down a little bottle of pills and say, "Here, take these."

Before he gives you medicine he says, "First of all, we'll find out what's wrong with you." Today, going to doctors usually involves an agonizing series of tests. They draw blood, take a urine sample, use different imaging techniques, put the whole picture together in order, they hope, to arrive at a diagnosis of what is wrong with you. A good doctor diagnoses your ailment, and then prescribes the treatment. It is futile to offer medicine to somebody until the problem has been diagnosed.

The Law is God's diagnostic instrument. He uses it to show us what is wrong with us. We return to Romans 3:20: "Therefore by the deeds of the law no flesh will be justified in His sight, for by the law is the knowledge of sin." What does the Law do? It makes us aware of sin. Paul adds, "What shall we say then? Is the law sin? Certainly not! On the contrary, I would not have known sin except through the law" (Romans 7:7). The only thing that revealed sin to Paul was the Law.

> Has then what is good become death to me? Certainly not! But sin, that it might appear sin, was producing death in me through what is good, so that sin through the commandment might become exceedingly sinful.
>
> verse 13

The purpose of the Commandments and ordinances was to bring sin out into the open and to reveal sin in its true nature as deceptive, destructive and deadly. Until we really see the nature of sin we are not going to see fully our need of salvation. You must know you are sick before you will be willing to take the doctor's remedy. Jesus said, "I didn't come to call the healthy, but the sick. I didn't come to call the righteous, but sinners" (see Matthew 9:12–13). The Law shows us the nature, operation and effects of sin, "so that sin through the commandment might become exceedingly sinful" (Romans 7:13). God gave the Law so that we would see this evil force of sin in all its horrible working and with all its deadly effects.

This is of particular interest to me because when I was a professional philosopher, my primary studies were in the philosophy of Plato, which I studied in great detail for many years. Plato was about the most intelligent man, by way of pure intellect, that I encountered in my studies. Basically, his philosophical theory was that knowledge is virtue. If only we know what is right, that is all we need. Well, that is obviously wrong, because lots of people know clearly what is right and still do what is wrong.

Is it not amazing that so great an intellect as Plato could not see that simple fact? Why did he not see it? Because he had nothing to reveal the nature of sin to him. He did not have the diagnostic, which is the Law of God. We should praise God every day for the revealed Word of God in the Bible, because it is the only book that offers us the correct diagnosis of our problem. Plato could not see the true nature of the human condition because he did not have the truth of the Bible available to him. The Law is given to bring sin out into the open and to show it in its true nature and character.

3. To Reveal Man's Carnal Nature

The third purpose for which the Law was given was to reveal man's carnal nature. Basically, our problems are the result of two forces at work within us. The first force is sin. I have spent years meditating on this truth, and in the light of both Scripture and experience, I believe that sin is an evil spiritual power at work in the universe. It is opposed to God, it is deceptive, and it is destructive.

In addition to that power, a second force is at work: a human nature that somehow comes under the influence of sin and turns away from the path of righteousness in acts of disobedience and rebellion. This is the carnal nature we inherited from Adam.

This nature is easily affected by sin. The Bible calls it "the old man," "the flesh," "the body," "the body of sin" or "the body of the sins of the flesh." Normally when Scripture uses these terms, it is not referring to the physical body, but rather to the nature we inherited with our physical body. Into every descendant of Adam there has been transmitted, by inheritance, a certain responsiveness to sin, a nature that is prone to rebel against God. The Law not only reveals sin; it also reveals the rebel inside. It is a perfect diagnostic. When we speak about man's carnal nature, therefore, we mean the rebel that is in each of us. Paul explains it this way:

> For we know that the law is spiritual, but I am carnal, sold under sin. [I am the slave of my own carnal nature.] For what I am doing, I do not understand. For what I will to do, that I do not practice; but what I hate, that I do.
>
> Romans 7:14–15

I am sure most of us have been able to identify with this passage at one time or another. The reality of this truth came to me with great force when I was fifteen years old and due to be confirmed in the Anglican Church. At that point I acknowledged that I needed to be a lot better than I was. So I decided that confirmation would be my turning point, and from then on I would become a really good person.

It was only when I decided to be good, however, that I discovered how bad I really was! Quite honestly, the harder I tried to be good, the quicker I got bad! After about six months I just gave it up. At the time, I had no idea that my problem was explained in the seventh chapter of Romans, and unfortunately there was no one there to tell me. But, what Paul states here was exactly my experience. "For what I am doing, I do not understand. For what I will to do, that I do not practice; but what I hate, that I do." It was the Law that made me conscious of the fact that I hated my sin. The Law pointed out what I should be doing. It said, "Do it." I said, "All right, I'll do it. Watch me." And, that is when the trouble started!

We see the conclusion of this dilemma in Romans 7:16–18:

> If, then, I do what I will not to do, I agree with the law that it is good. [I say the Law is good.] But now, it is no longer I who do it, but sin that dwells in me. [The Law brings sin out into the open.] For I know that in me (that is, in my flesh) [my carnal nature] nothing good dwells; for to will is present with me, but how to perform what is good I do not find.

The Law has laid bare the power of sin and my carnal nature. It brings out into the light the two root problems of my life.

4. To Foreshadow Christ

The fourth purpose of the Law is to foreshadow Christ. Not only does the Law diagnose the problem, it foreshows the solution. In Luke's gospel we read the words Jesus spoke to a group of His disciples after His resurrection when they were still slow to believe that He had risen from the dead:

> Then He said to them, "O foolish ones, and slow of heart to believe in all that the prophets have spoken! Ought not the Christ to have suffered these things and to enter into His glory?" And beginning at Moses and all the Prophets, He expounded to them in all the Scriptures the things concerning Himself.
>
> Luke 24:25–27

Jesus continues the same thought in verse 44:

> Then He said to them, "These are the words which I spoke to you while I was still with you, that all things must be fulfilled which were written in the Law of Moses and the Prophets and the Psalms concerning Me."

Jesus, being a good Jew, enumerates the three sections of the Jewish Tanakh, commonly referred to as the Old Testament. The Hebrew Scriptures are divided into three sections: the *Torah*, the Law of Moses (Genesis through Deuteronomy); *Nevi'im*, most of the prophets (which include some of the books of history); and *Ketuvim*, which are the other writings. Thus, when Jesus refers to the Law, the Prophets and the writings, He is saying that all these foreshowed Him.

One of the major purposes of the Law, therefore, with its prophecies and with all its sacrifices, was to foreshow Christ. When your eyes are opened by the Holy Spirit, every sacrifice in the Law of Moses is a revelation of Jesus Christ. There is not a single exception.

5. To Bring Us to Christ

The fifth purpose of the Law was to bring us to Christ: "Therefore the law was our tutor to bring us to Christ, that we might be justified by faith" (Galatians 3:24). The Greek word for *tutor* is *paidagogos*, which gives us the English word *pedagogue*. The meaning of the Greek word, however, is different from the English *pedagogue*, which is a teacher or schoolmaster. In the Greek and Roman civilization of Paul's day, a wealthy father would have a senior trusted slave who would be charged with the initial education of the children. Before these children were old enough to go to school, the *paidagogos* would take them under his charge and train them in the basic principles of obedience, good behavior and right and wrong. Then, when they became old enough to go to the school with a formal teacher, he would accompany them to the school and deliver them to the teacher.

Generally, this senior slave would be rather strict and severe with the children—usually, more strict and severe than the father himself would have been. Paul says the Law was this senior slave to us. Its work was to teach us the basic principles of righteousness, of obedience, of right and wrong, and then to take us to the real teacher, who is Christ.

6. To Keep Israel a Separate People

The sixth purpose of the Law was to keep Israel a separate nation, shut up unto the purposes of God, which were to be fulfilled in Christ. Returning to Galatians 3 we read this: "But before faith came, we were kept under guard by the law, kept for the faith which would afterward be revealed" (verse 23). The Law of Moses has kept the Jews a separate group of people for two thousand years. No matter where Jews go—the United States, Arabia, Latin America, Great Britain—it does not matter; they are kept shut up because God still has a purpose for them.

In Numbers 23:9, we read the words of Balaam as he gives a prophetic vision of Israel:

> For from the top of the rocks I see him,
> And from the hills I behold him;
> There! A people dwelling alone,
> Not reckoning itself among the nations.

The word *nations* is the Hebrew word *goyim*, the word for Gentile. Even after Israel has been driven out of her own land for two thousand years, this prophecy has been fulfilled concerning the Jewish people. "A people dwelling alone, not reckoning itself among the nations." It is one of the most remarkable facts of history that the Jewish nation could still be a separate identifiable people after being dispersed from its own land for nineteen centuries, scattered among at least one hundred other nations.

My first wife, Lydia, was Danish and she often said to me, "If you scattered the Danes amongst the other nations and came back at the end of a hundred years, you wouldn't find a single Dane." The unique ability to maintain their national identity is true only of Israel. And what kept them separate was primarily the Law of Moses.

Observing the Law has always separated the Jews out from other people. They have kept the Law at tremendous personal cost and sacrifice to themselves, but God has kept them separate to wait for their Messiah to come.

In summary, here are six purposes for which God gave the Law:

1. *Not* as a means to achieve righteousness
2. To reveal sin
3. To reveal man's carnal nature
4. To foreshadow Christ
5. To bring us to Christ
6. To keep Israel a separate people

Even though the Law cannot make us righteous before God, every human being naturally feels that the way to be righteous is to try to do just that. We put our faith in the Law, assuming that succeeding in at least some part of it helps us stay in right standing. We do not realize that this has serious consequences.

If the Law was not given to achieve righteousness, then, how does the Law affect me if I try to keep it? We consider this question in detail in the next chapter.

4

The Effects of Law

The effect of the Law on those who try to keep it is one of the most astonishing themes I have ever studied anywhere in the Bible. I actually went over it several times to convince myself I had gotten it right. When you read through the list, it should cure you forever of wanting to live by religious law.

What does the Law do in people? I believe the New Testament indicates there are at least nine results the Law brings to us if we come under its influence.

1. The Law Stirs Up Sin

The first effect the Law has upon us is to stir up sin: "When we were in the flesh, the sinful passions which were aroused by the law were at work in our members to bear fruit to death" (Romans 7:5).

What enables the passions of sin to work in our flesh? The Law. What stirs up sin? The Law. I believe Romans 7:9 to be one of the most extraordinary statements in the Bible: "I was alive once without the law, but when the commandment came, sin revived and I died." I have spent years meditating on this verse, wondering what Paul could have meant. I will offer here three possible ways of interpreting this statement, and you may freely take your choice as to which you prefer.

One interpretation might be that Paul is a descendant of Adam, as you and I are, and he is talking about himself, in Adam, saying in so many words, "I was alive in Adam to God, but when the commandment came it brought sin to light and I died."

If there had never been any commandment, Adam would never have sinned. Have you ever thought about that? If God had put Adam in the Garden without any restrictions, Adam could not have sinned. But when Adam was confronted with a commandment, that was what prompted sin. So, Paul was alive, in Adam, without the commandment just as we all were. When the commandment came, however, sin came to life, and we died.

Another possible interpretation is that Paul was speaking as an Israelite. Israel was delivered from the bondage of Egypt not by the Law, but by grace through faith in the blood of the Passover Lamb. The Law came about fifty days after the Exodus. Up to that time, Israel was alive unto God as a redeemed people saved by grace. But when the Law came, the first thing they did was worship the golden calf. They immediately broke the First Commandment. What caused that? The Commandment. What did the Commandment do? Stirred up sin. Sin had been dormant until the Commandment came.

God delivered them by grace, but He tested them. He said, "Now, what are you going to do? Are you going to go on by grace, or are you going to earn your way to the Promised Land?" They said, in so many words, "We'll earn it." And, in the course of the next few days, disaster came. Up to this point in their journey, there was no barrier between Israel and God until they said, "We'll earn it." Then God said to Moses, "Put bounds around the mountain. Don't let the people come near." The Law does not bring people near to God. It keeps them away from God.

How foolish Israel was! They could have gone on in grace all the way to the Promised Land. How foolish you and I can be as well! My conviction is that there is hardly a single Christian who at some point in his or her experience has not made the same mistake. We are saved by grace and then we determine we are going to earn our way. Then what happens? We lose our joy, we lose our peace, and we become a slave again. If we continue, we become nasty, edgy, critical, religious people whom no one cares to be around.

Let me suggest one more interpretation of Paul's statement. If ever anybody was saved by grace, it was the apostle Paul. There he was on the road to Damascus, just about to abuse every follower of Jesus he could find. Right in the middle of the journey Jesus sovereignly revealed Himself to Paul. Paul did not ask Him to do it, Jesus just did it out of grace.

What I am about to suggest I cannot prove, and I will not attempt to do so. We know, however, that after a while Paul went back to Tarsus, and if it had not been for Barnabas we might never have heard of the apostle Paul—because it was Barnabas who went to Tarsus and found him. I believe that Paul had returned to Tarsus and had become a good, regular attendant in the synagogue. I think there is a possibility that he placed himself back under the Law in some measure. Why? *Because* there were no riots in Tarsus; nobody tried to stone Paul in Tarsus; and, there is no record of any trouble there. The Jews never objected to preaching the Law, but they always fought violently against the message of grace. When Paul said, therefore, that he was once alive apart from the Law, I believe he may have been referring to his initial experience in grace. But when he came back under the Law, sin again became alive and he "died."

Over the years, I have come to the conclusion that we may consider coming back under the Law to be the isolated experience of only a few legalistic people. On the contrary, however, I believe it is actually *the* great danger that threatens every believer. We are saved by grace and then after a little while we think, *Now I'm living a really clean life, I've learned a lot of very valuable principles, I know the Scripture, and I have my quiet time every morning. I can walk in victory by my own efforts.* Clearly, the end of this kind of thinking is a disaster. Endeavoring to live the Christian life by your own efforts is the greatest single hindrance to walking in the Spirit.

Romans 8 is a wonderful picture of the Spirit-filled life. One series of messages, which I taught on the book of Romans, was called "The Roman Pilgrimage," and showed how Romans 8 is the goal of the journey that Paul lays out in the first seven chapters of his epistle.

In these messages I compare the journey into the Spirit-filled life to the old-fashioned coffee percolator. Now, you might remember instant coffee. Say what you like, but no television commercial was ever going to convince me that instant was as good as perked coffee! Similarly, many people want instant holiness and instant liberty by jumping from Romans 1 into Romans 8. I do not believe it works that way. If you want to live in Romans 8, you must forget any thought of "instant results" and enter through "the percolator," which is Romans 2, 3, 4, 5, 6 and 7, because there is something to deal with in every chapter. The last phase of the percolating process is Romans 7, which deals with the problem of the Law.

For years I could not understand why Paul devotes a whole chapter to dealing with the Law right in the middle of Romans, immediately after grace had been so clearly set forth. I have found, however, that his progression is true to experience. Paul deals with sin in Romans 3 and in Romans 6 he deals with the old man. We would like to think that this is the end, but it is not. The final hurdle you have to clear is the Law, and in some ways it may be the most difficult.

Looking back over my life, I think it took me at least thirty years to clear the hurdle of the Law. It is only in my later years that I have begun to feel I have some concept of grace. It is my hope that those in generations to follow will not take so long. In my case, I believe my understanding of law vs. grace came because I learned my lessons the slow, hard way.

2. The Law Strengthens Sin

The second fact about the Law is that it strengthens sin. This point is similar to the first, so we will not dwell extensively on it. In 1 Corinthians 15:56, we read, "The sting of death is sin, and the strength of sin is the law." Do you really understand this statement? It is almost frightening. Did you know that grace frightens people? They think: *You mean I don't have a set of rules to keep? What will I do?* They feel kind of naked, alone and unsure of where to go.

A second verse, which we have looked at before, is Romans 6:14: "For sin shall not have dominion over you, for you are not under law but under grace." If you are under the Law, sin *will* have dominion over you, because it is the Law that strengthens the dominion of sin over you.

3. The Law Produces Transgression and Wrath

The third fact about the Law is that it produces transgression, which leads to wrath. Romans 4:15 contains two statements that we need to examine carefully: "The law brings about wrath; for where there is no law there is no transgression." *To transgress* means to step over a line that has been marked out. The Law marks out a line and says, "You mustn't step beyond this." Where the line has not been marked out, there can be no transgression. You are not a transgressor without the Law.

And transgression, Paul says, produces *wrath* on the part of the one against whom we transgress. So the Law produces transgression and, therefore, divine wrath.

I like to illustrate this by a kind of familiar incident that could be taken from anybody's family. Mother goes out for a little while on a Sunday afternoon, and leaves little Sarah Jane at home with Dad on the sofa watching the game. When Mother comes back, she discovers that Sarah Jane has sneaked upstairs and not only gotten into every one of her face creams but polished her good leather shoes with them. Of course, Mother is upset. But after all, Sarah Jane did not know any better. So Mommy just says, "Don't do that again," and the whole incident is over with.

The next time Mother goes out she pauses in the doorway and wags her finger at Sarah Jane and says, "Now remember, don't you touch my face creams." Well, of course, Sarah Jane, being like you and me, is interested in only one thing from that moment onward: the face creams! So back comes Mother from her outing, and her expensive creams are once again smeared on her leather shoes. Can you guess Mother's reaction? It is wrath! She is mad. And can you guess whether or not Sarah Jane is punished?

You see, if there is no Law, there is no transgression. The Law produces transgression and, therefore, wrath. Likewise, if the Law is removed, there is no longer any place for transgression.

4. The Law Causes Condemnation

Fourth, the Law causes condemnation. In the opening verses of Romans 8, Paul writes: "There is therefore now no condemnation to those who are in Christ Jesus. . . . For what the law could not do in that it was weak through the flesh, God did by sending His own Son" (Romans 8:1, 3).

In other words, the Law can never set you free from condemnation; it can only bring you under condemnation. We should note here that the first step—the primary requirement for living the Spirit-filled life of Romans 8—is in verse 1: "There is therefore now no condemnation." As long as you live under condemnation, you cannot live in liberty. Anybody who is under condemnation is really the prey of the devil and does not know true spiritual liberty. Before you can enter into liberty, condemnation must be abolished once and for all. And, condemnation can only be abolished by dealing with the problem of the Law, which is Paul's point in Romans 7.

5. The Law Keeps Us under Satan's Dominion

Fifth, the Law keeps us under Satan's dominion. Colossians 2:14–16 reveals what God accomplished through the death of Christ on the cross.

> . . . having wiped out the handwriting of requirements [that is, the Law] that was against us, which was contrary to us. And He has taken it out of the way, having nailed it to the cross. Having disarmed principalities and powers . . .

God annulled the Law through the death of Jesus, and having done that, these verses confirm that He disarmed the principalities and powers. The principalities and powers are Satan's spiritual dominating forces. Jesus stripped them of their ability to dominate us. How? He revoked the Law. As long as we were under the Law we were guilty; and as long as we were guilty, we were under Satan's dominion. We have to be delivered from the obligation of the Law before we can be delivered from the dominion of Satan. As long as we are under the Law, we are under the dominion of Satan.

Some of these statements will seem shocking, because, remember, every human being feels inherently that the way to be righteous is to keep the Law. We just need to meditate on the truths of the grace of God until they become real to us. A radical transformation must take place inside us before we will abandon our faith in the Law.

6. The Law Brings a Curse

Sixth, the Law brings a curse:

> For as many as are of the works of the law are under the curse; for it is written, "Cursed is everyone who does not continue in all things which are written in the book of the law, to do them."
>
> Galatians 3:10

If you are under the Law, you must do the *whole Law, all the time.* If you do not, you are under a curse: "Thus says the LORD: 'Cursed is the man who trusts in man and makes flesh his strength, whose heart departs from the LORD'" (Jeremiah 17:5).

I believe this verse expresses the essence of *legalism*. Basically, legalism is the attempt to achieve righteousness with God by keeping a set of rules; it is adding to what God has required for righteousness. Like the Galatians, we who have known the Lord, tasted His grace, experienced His supernatural power and found deliverance from sin go back to trusting in our own ability and our own rules. In so doing, *our hearts depart from the Lord*. The vital point to see is that by reverting to a dependence upon the Law, we come under a curse.

In my opinion, this is the condition of most professing Christians in the Church today. Almost every significant movement in the Church began in the power of the Holy Spirit. Today, however, many are relying on the flesh; they are relying on their own efforts, programs, promotions and rules. This results in the curse that is described in the next verse: "For he shall be like a shrub in the desert, and shall not see when good comes, but shall inhabit the parched places in the wilderness, in a salt land which is not inhabited" (Jeremiah 17:6).

This vividly describes someone under a curse. The man or woman under a curse is like a bush in the desert. Blessing comes all around—prosperity, liberty and freedom—but like this little bush, they never feel the rain or enjoy the greenness because they are under a curse. The most common reason why Christians come under a curse is legalism, which is one of the primary themes of Galatians. Paul began chapter 3 of

The Effects of Law

Galatians with the surprising statement, "O foolish Galatians! Who has bewitched you?"

How does Paul know they are bewitched? They have lost their vision of Jesus on the cross, which is the source of grace and justification. They had begun in faith and in the power of the Holy Spirit, but now they are seeking to become perfect in the flesh. This is legalism: seeking to become righteous by keeping law. Remember, if you are going to be justified by the Law, you must keep the whole Law, all the time, or you come under a curse. My advice: Do not try to keep the Law, because you certainly will not succeed!

7. The Law Brings a Double Enmity

The Law produces a double enmity. Look again at these verses from Ephesians:

> For He [Jesus Christ] Himself is our peace, who has made both [Jew and Gentile] one, and has broken down the middle wall of separation, having abolished in His flesh the enmity, that is, the law of commandments contained in ordinances, so as to create in Himself one new man from the two, thus making peace, and that He might reconcile them both to God in one body through the cross, thereby putting to death the enmity.
>
> Ephesians 2:14–16

Looking closely at this Scripture we see there is a double enmity produced by the Law. As we have already seen, the

67

Law produces enmity between God and man, because if we are under the Law but do not keep it, we become transgressors.

In verse 15, however, when Paul talks about the enmity, he is not talking about enmity between man and God. He is talking about enmity between those under the Law and those not under the Law. This, in my opinion, is the basic problem of the Jewish people.

I remember talking to an official of the Hebrew University who was my Hebrew teacher in 1947, just before the State of Israel came into being. He was explaining to me (which was the traditionally accepted Jewish point of view) that the problem of the Jews being persecuted was because they were just a peculiar, separated minority wherever they were in the world. His belief was that once the Jews returned to Israel and had their own country, the enmity would cease.

"Well," I said, "if the enmity is purely sociological, you may be right. But if it's spiritual, you'll be wrong." I believe he was indeed wrong, because the enmity toward Israel has never ceased. The root problem is that the Law separates one company of people and distinguishes them from all others. Those who keep the Law feel in their hearts they are superior to other people who do not keep the Law, and that produces enmity.

Before I became a Christian, I was what you would call an educated, sophisticated Britisher. But as a Gentile, I had in my mind a deep, underlying mistrust of the Jewish people. As I came to know the Jewish people better, I learned that in the heart of the Jews is a deep underlying mistrust of the Gentiles. It is a mutual enmity, which, Paul says, is caused by the Law.

68

Let me give you a simple illustration of how this works. At one point my wife, Ruth, and I went on the Weight Watchers diet. This diet was very disciplined then. Everything had to be measured right down to the last leaf of lettuce. But Weight Watchers worked! I would endorse it anywhere as a means of slimming down—if you kept it up.

After about a month, I was losing weight and I began to observe my inner reactions. I walked around with a rather superior attitude, looking at other people and thinking, *They ought to be on Weight Watchers.* Have you ever noticed that the successful follower of a diet program is a real evangelist? He or she will go everywhere and tell anybody who will listen, "I'm on such-and-such diet. Look what it has done for me. I lost two pounds last week."

One day as I was considering this, I thought to myself, *What about the Jews? They've been leading a peculiar, separated life with different diets and different laws for three thousand, five hundred years!* Can you imagine what living under such a separate system of laws has done to them? It is no wonder they struggle to come out from under such a deeply ingrained lifestyle. This is one of the reasons why the Jews find themselves at enmity with the world and the world with them. The Law produces enmity. It divides God from man and man from his fellow man.

8. The Law Produces Bondage

The Law produces bondage. Many translations usually use the word *bondage,* but I prefer *slavery,* which is a more vivid translation of the Greek word. In the fourth chapter of Galatians, Paul is writing to Christians who are trying to come under, or, in the case of the Jews, come back under, the Law of Moses. To help them understand what they are doing, he uses an allegory:

> Tell me, you who desire to be under the law, do you not hear the law? For it is written that Abraham had two sons: the one by a bondwoman, the other by a freewoman. But he who was of the bondwoman was born according to the flesh, and he of the freewoman through promise, which things are symbolic. For these are the two covenants: the one from Mount Sinai which gives birth to bondage, which is Hagar—for this Hagar is Mount Sinai in Arabia, and corresponds to Jerusalem which now is, and is in bondage with her children.
>
> Galatians 4:21–25

In this allegory Paul compares Abraham's two wives and two sons: Hagar, who was the mother of Ishmael; and Sarah, who was the mother of Isaac. In this allegory, he says that Hagar corresponds to the covenant of the Law made on Sinai, and Ishmael corresponds to the works of the flesh, or of the Law. Hagar was a slave woman and, therefore, produced a slave. This, he says, corresponds to the earthly Jerusalem of his day, which was in bondage under the Law. Paul is warning the Galatians that if they come under the Law, they will come under bondage.

Paul says the same thing when he tells the believers in Rome to continue in a life of grace and not go back under the Law: "For as many as are led by the Spirit of God, these are sons of God. For you did not receive the spirit of bondage again to fear" (Romans 8:14–15).

In describing legalism this way, Paul is warning the Roman Christians not to go back under bondage to religious Law. All who do, he says, will become slaves to fear. Remember, the Law says, "Do this! If you don't do this, you're a sinner. Don't do that! If you do that, you'll go to hell." The Law uses fear to motivate us. For many centuries the basic motivation of Christian preaching (both Catholic and Protestant) has been fear. We have become so used to that kind of motivation that we believe religion is supposed to be a fearful existence. The New Testament message, however, is not a message of fear.

9. The Law Produces Persecutors

Finally, the last effect of the Law is that it produces persecutors. We return to the book of Galatians, where Paul continues the parallel between law and grace using the allegory of Ishmael and Isaac. "But, as he who was born according to the flesh [Ishmael] then persecuted him who was born according to the Spirit [Isaac], even so it is now" (Galatians 4:29).

If you are a child of God walking in the Spirit, your persecutors will be the religionists, the people who know only religious law. You will offend them, you will frighten them, and they will get angry.

The reaction of the religious legalist to grace can be bizarre. When John Wesley went throughout England preaching the Gospel of free grace, he preached in Cornwall and a man there received what the Methodists call "assurance." This man suddenly believed (and in those days it was a very hard thing to believe) that his sins were forgiven. The church people in the late 1700s were so used to religious legalism that the concept of actually knowing your sins were forgiven was astonishing. It took Wesley years to achieve that assurance for himself.

The man who received assurance of the forgiveness went around testifying that he knew his sins were forgiven. It may be surprising for us to think that statement would disturb people, but it turned the whole community against him. They persecuted him to the point of press-ganging him into the British Navy. He was forced into naval service, leaving his wife and children behind. Why? Because he simply told people he knew his sins were forgiven and it scared the whole religious community. Grace always frightens and offends legalism, and the religious legalist will always react with some form of persecution.

When we walk in grace, it is not the secular world we need to fear. The persecutors of those who walked the way of grace were those who kept the Law. Who persecuted Jesus and the apostles? The religious legalists. Who has persecuted the true witnesses of Jesus for more than twenty centuries? The religious legalists. It is Ishmael who persecutes Isaac, and it will be so to the end of the age. As we saw in our first chapter, Cain murdered Abel because Cain was under the Law and Abel was walking in grace and faith. Cain was the product of the flesh, and the flesh and the spirit are at enmity.

Let's end this section with a review of the effects of the Law:

1. The Law stirs up sin.
2. The Law strengthens sin.
3. The Law produces transgression and therefore wrath.
4. The Law causes condemnation.
5. The Law keeps us under Satan's dominion.
6. The Law brings a curse.
7. The Law produces a double enmity: between God and man; and between those under the Law and those not under the Law.
8. The Law produces slavery.
9. The Law produces persecutors.

The Root: Self-Dependence

After reviewing all the effects of the Law we might understandably ask, "Well, why then the Law? If the Law just produces all these problems, why did God ever get us involved in the Law? What is its ultimate purpose?" As I indicated earlier, I believe the Law is God's divine diagnostic. God intends through the Law to lay bare our root problem, which I believe can be summed up in one phrase: *self-dependence.*

The hardest tendency to curtail in our own lives is depending upon ourselves. I believe the inner motivation of sin, in its essence, is the desire to be independent of God. In Genesis 3:5, we read the temptation of Satan that persuaded Eve and, therefore, Adam to disobey God: "For God knows that in the day you eat of it your eyes will be opened, and you will be like God, knowing good and evil."

Is it wrong to desire to be like God? We could easily understand if Satan had tempted Eve to commit adultery or murder. We know that is wrong. But what is wrong with wanting to be like God? I would have to say it all depends on your motive. What Satan said in essence was, "If you know the difference between good and evil, you'll no longer need to *depend upon God*. You can make your own decisions and run your own life." The essence of Adam and Eve's sin was the desire not to depend on God any longer. That desire to be independent from God is the root in every ego. It is the desire to do my own thing, to go my own way.

The one person who perfectly sets forth the opposite of the desire to be independent is Jesus. He said, "The Son can do nothing of Himself . . . the living Father sent Me, and I live because of the Father" (John 5:19; 6:57). (See also John 5:30.) The picture of Jesus is total, continuing dependence on His Father. That is also what God wants of every child of His. The great enemy is self-dependence and self-reliance as we discovered earlier: "Cursed is the man who trusts in man and makes flesh his strength, whose heart departs from the LORD" (Jeremiah 17:5).

What is the essence of Jeremiah's charge against Israel? The one who trusts in himself makes flesh his strength (relies on his own carnal nature), and in so doing, his heart departs from the Lord. The result is more flesh, as Jesus says: "That which is born of the flesh is flesh" (John 3:6). In essence, He is saying that flesh can only beget flesh. If we rely on our own efforts all we ever propagate is more flesh.

74

This is such a critical point that I want to expand it as we close this chapter. Habakkuk 2:4 is a key verse of the Bible. This is the verse on which Paul bases his doctrine of justification by faith. It is quoted three times in the New Testament: in Romans 1:17, Galatians 3:11 and Hebrews 10:38. The latter part of the verse is quoted in the New Testament, but for our purposes, look at the entire verse: "Behold the proud, his soul is not upright in him; but the just shall live by his faith" (Habakkuk 2:4).

For many years I could not understand how the two halves of that verse fit together. Then God opened my eyes and I realized that what is presented there are two alternatives. You can humble yourself and in faith depend on the Lord, or you can trust in yourself and your soul will be lifted up in arrogant religious pride. There are only those two alternatives. Everyone is in one category or the other.

Paul concludes, "Where is boasting then? It is excluded. By what law? Of works? No, but by the law of faith" (Romans 3:27). If I am always doing the right thing in my own strength, I can boast. But if I am simply trusting in the grace of God and depending upon Him, I have nothing to boast of. Faith excludes boasting.

He also applies this to the nation of Israel: "For they [Israel] being ignorant of God's righteousness, and seeking to establish their own righteousness, have not submitted to the righteousness of God" (Romans 10:3).

If we, like Israel, are seeking to establish our own righteousness, we are not submitted to the righteousness of God. The root of seeking our own righteousness is pride. A Jew of Paul's day could boast, "I don't need God's grace. I keep the six hundred and thirteen commandments of Judaism." If you watch, you will notice that religious people will always multiply commandments because it inflates their ego. They can boast, "My dear friend, you have only Ten Commandments. What's that? I have six hundred. I spend my life worrying about my six hundred commandments—and look how religious I am."

Writing to the Christians at Corinth, Paul says: "For you see your calling, brethren, that not many wise according to the flesh, not many mighty, not many noble, are called" (1 Corinthians 1:26). God has no prejudice against people who are wise or mighty or noble. He loves them all. Why, then, was only a small proportion of the wise or mighty or noble in Corinth submitted to God? It is because those who are wise, mighty or noble normally trust in themselves.

Here is a list of five things that we commonly trust in rather than depending on the grace of God.

1. Wealth.
2. Nobility or social position.
3. Education or knowledge. Note that knowledge was the original temptation. "You will be like God, knowing good and evil" (Genesis 3:5). You will not need God because you will have enough knowledge in yourself.
4. Power.
5. Religion. And religion is the biggest stumbling block of all. "I have my religion. Why do I need grace? I'm a good Lutheran, Catholic or charismatic. Why do I need the grace of God?" Do you think people are not like that? Believe me, churches are full of people like that.

I offer you a final thought on this subject. Jesus spoke these words: "And even now the ax is laid to the root of the trees" (Matthew 3:10). The root spoken of here is self-dependence. God gave the Law to lay bare that root of self-dependence, and the Gospel of grace puts the ax to it. But, obviously, if you have not laid the root bare, you cannot lay the ax to it.

It took me more than thirty years to clear away all the religious language and institutionalism and get down to what matters—which is depending on the grace of God. I trust that you, by the grace of God, will not take as long.

Two Closing Questions

At this point in our study we have established that we are not required to keep the Law of Moses, and that, in fact, we are not made righteous by keeping any form of religious law. The Law was given to be *God's diagnostic*—to show that the inner motivation of sin is the *desire to be independent of God*. Whenever this desire is present, the result is sin. Thus, the Law was given to expose our root problem, *self-dependence*. Grace through the Gospel lays the ax to that root.

Two logical questions, therefore, confront us. The first is, *If we are not to keep the Law, what does God require of us?* The second is, *How does God enable us to do what He requires?* Simply put, the two questions we must answer are *what* and *how*. We will consider these questions in the following chapters.

5

The Righteousness God Requires

What does God require of us as Christians living under grace rather than under the religious laws?

I am sure we all understand that we do not have to be circumcised, to observe new moons and Sabbaths or to make offerings of meal, wine, goats or sheep—which were all requirements of the Law of Moses. But the question of what to do remains. It is an important question and, surprisingly, I find few Christians who have given much serious thought to the answer. As a result, they get involved in religious routines and go on doing what they have always done.

The Righteous Requirement of the Law

Let's begin by looking in Romans. You will remember my statement that Romans 8 is the picture of the Spirit-filled life.

> For what the law could not do in that it was weak through the flesh, God did by sending His own Son in the likeness of sinful flesh, on account of sin: He condemned sin in the flesh, that the righteous requirement of the law might be fulfilled in us who do not walk according to the flesh but according to the Spirit.
>
> Romans 8:3–4

What the Law could not do, God did another way. Paul is always careful to point out that there was nothing wrong with the Law; he states that the Law is "holy and just and good" (Romans 7:12). The weakness is in our human flesh: We are unable to keep the Law. In fact, as we have clearly seen, when our carnal nature is confronted with the Law, the result is rebellion. When we try to keep the Law we actually become worse than we were when we did not bother about it. The fault is not in the Law; we are the problem. Because of man's carnal nature, therefore, God had to find another way to accomplish His purposes.

To do that, God sent His own Son in the likeness of sinful flesh, and condemned our sin in the flesh of Jesus Christ on the cross. There on the cross God executed our carnal nature, dealt with sin, dealt with the flesh and opened the way to a new solution. The outworking of the alternative is described in Romans 8:4: "That the righteous requirement of the law might be fulfilled in us who do not walk according to the flesh [we are no longer living in the old carnal nature] but according to the Spirit."

The key phrase here is "*the righteous requirement of the law.*" In the New Testament there are two main Greek words for *righteousness*. One is *dikaiosune,* which means "abstract righteousness," in other words, not connected with any particular act or person. The other is *dikaioma.* This is the word Paul uses and it means "righteousness worked out in action." Thus, we are not required to keep the Law, but we are expected to produce the outworked righteousness of the Law.

Now the question becomes, *What is the outworked righteousness of the Law?* We could ask that question another way: *What was the righteousness that the Law was intended to accomplish but could not produce?* The answer is amazingly simple. We see it in Matthew 22:35–40, which records an incident in the closing week of the ministry of Jesus in Jerusalem when He was confronted and questioned by the Jewish religious leaders: "Then one of them, a lawyer, asked Him a question" (verse 35).

When you read the word *lawyer* in the New Testament, do not think about an attorney. The proper translation is "a theologian." This man was a student of religious law. God has nothing against attorneys, God bless them. I wonder, however, if He may have a few things against theologians. "Then one of them, a [theologian], asked Him a question, testing Him, and saying, 'Teacher, which is the great commandment in the law?'" (verses 35–36).

Notice, Jesus did not hedge or reject the question. He gave an immediate, specific, final answer.

> Jesus said to him, "'You shall love the LORD your God with all your heart, with all your soul, and with all your mind.' This is the first and great commandment. And the second is like it: 'You shall love your neighbor as yourself.' On these two commandments hang all the Law and the Prophets."
>
> verses 37–40

Love—the Requirement of the Law

Here is a simple illustration of what Jesus means when He uses the word *hang*. If I come into my home and hang my jacket on a peg next to the door, one fact is obvious: The peg must be there before I hang my jacket on it. Jesus says that the entire Old Testament is hung on two objectives—love for God and love for my neighbor. And if the Law and the Prophets are hung on those two commandments, then those two commandments had to be there *before* the Law and the Prophets. These two commandments encompass the basic, eternal, unchanging requirements of God: Love God, and love your neighbor. *This is the righteous requirement of the Law.*

This requirement is repeated throughout the New Testament. We see it, for instance, in Romans:

> Owe no one anything except to love one another, for he who loves another has fulfilled the law. For the commandments,

"You shall not commit adultery," "You shall not murder,"
"You shall not steal," "You shall not bear false witness," "You
shall not covet," and if there is any other commandment,
are all summed up in this saying, namely, "You shall love
your neighbor as yourself." Love does no harm to a neighbor;
therefore love is the fulfillment of the law.

Romans 13:8–10

Paul here makes a completely uncompromising, specific
statement: "Love is the fulfillment of the Law." This is restated in Galatians 5:14, "For all the law is fulfilled in one
word, even in this: 'You shall love your neighbor as yourself.'"

Let me point out how important it is to love yourself. If you
do not love yourself, what is the good of loving your neighbor
the way you love—or do not love—yourself? The root of this
failure to love ourselves is rejection and inferiority, both of
which have no place in Christian living.

Looking further on in Galatians 5:22–23 we read: "But the
fruit of the Spirit is love, joy, peace, longsuffering, kindness,
goodness, faithfulness, gentleness, self-control. Against such
there is no law." People who are living in the fruit of the Spirit
do not need to be controlled by a law. There is no law given
by God that will ever prevent a person from doing what the
fruit of the Spirit would lead him or her to do.

Finally, we look at 1 Timothy 1:5: "Now the purpose of
the commandment is love from a pure heart, from a good
conscience, and from sincere faith." The word *commandment* is an unfortunate translation. I would prefer to translate
it this way: *the final objective of our message.* Paul says
the primary purpose of all his preaching is summed up in

83

one word—*love*. Any kind of religious activity, teaching or preaching that is not aimed at producing love is missing the mark of God's ultimate purpose.

Having established this point, Paul adds: "Some, having strayed, have turned aside to idle talk, desiring to be teachers of the law, understanding neither what they say nor the things which they affirm" (1 Timothy 1:6–7).

Any religious teaching that is not aimed at producing love—however wonderful it may seem—is just empty talk. In addition, Paul adds that many people desire to be teachers of the Law, but they do not understand the nature of the Law, the purpose of the Law or the problems of the Law.

Then, Paul makes this wonderful statement: "But we know that the law is good if one uses it lawfully, knowing this: that the law is not made for a righteous person" (1 Timothy 1:8–9).

At this point you must ask yourself, "Have I been made righteous by faith in Christ?" If you have not, then your faith in Christ has done you no good. But, if you have been made righteous by your faith in Christ, then the Law is not made for you. You cannot have it both ways. The problem with many Christians is that they really are not sure whether they are righteous or not. The Bible makes this distinction clear: "Therefore, having been justified [made righteous] by faith, we have peace with God" (Romans 5:1).

If you have been made righteous by faith in Jesus Christ, the Law is not for you because the Law is not given for a righteous person. If you think, *Well, I believe I'm safer under the Law because I'll know what to do*, then read further and you will see for whom the Law is made:

84

[The Law is made] for the lawless and insubordinate, for the ungodly and for sinners, for the unholy and profane, for murderers of fathers and murderers of mothers, for manslayers, for fornicators, for sodomites [homosexuals], for kidnappers, for liars, for perjurers.

1 Timothy 1:9–10

You must choose which of the two categories you wish to belong to. Do you wish to belong with the righteous, or with the murderers of fathers and mothers, the fornicators and the kidnappers? God has not given us a third category. The issue is very clear. Either we are made righteous by faith or we are not. If you believe you have been made righteous by faith, then the Law is not for you.

Motivated by Love

The following statement may shock you, but as we examine the Scriptures together, I believe you will come to agree with it. *The person motivated purely by love is always free to do exactly what he wants, and, thus, lives like a king.* It may be surprising that our primary text for this statement is found in the book of James. Some people think James believed in the Law and in works, but I believe this verse indicates that James and Paul are of one accord on these issues: "He who looks into the perfect law of liberty [or freedom] and continues in it, and is not a forgetful hearer but a doer of the work, this one will be blessed in what he does" (James 1:25). The

85

Gospel presents to us the perfect law, which is the law of liberty, the law of freedom.

Then James continues this theme: "If you really fulfill the royal [or kingly] law according to the Scripture, 'You shall love your neighbor as yourself,' you do well" (James 2:8).

James designates this law of the Gospel in two ways: "the law of liberty [or freedom]" and "the royal [or kingly] law." Why? Because when you are motivated only by pure love, you can always do exactly what you want to do. There are no restrictions. Additionally, a man or woman who can always do exactly what he or she wants to do is free and lives like a king. This is the life the Gospel presents: *freedom and kingship through love.*

God's Requirements Never Change

God's primary requirements of righteousness have never varied from age to age or from race to race. Most Christians seem to believe that somewhere in the middle of human history God changed His mind about what He expected of humankind. These people believe that up to a certain point, God expected man to be warlike, destroying cities and putting people to death. Then suddenly, in the middle of history, God changed His mind and said, "No, what I really want is love and peace." This line of thinking is a caricature of Scripture's revelations, when, in fact, God has maintained the same requirements since the beginning.

In John's gospel and his first epistle, he writes about *the beginning.* Whenever John uses this phrase, he is referring to the opening chapters of Genesis. The Hebrew title for Genesis is *bereshith*, which means "in the beginning." *Bereshith* is also the first word of Genesis. At the opening of John's gospel, therefore, when he writes *in the beginning*, he is referring to Genesis 1:1. In his first epistle when he uses this phrase *the beginning*, he is referring to the same thing.

> Brethren, I write no new commandment to you, but an old commandment which you have had from the beginning [from Genesis 1:1]. The old commandment is the word [of God] which you heard from the beginning.
>
> 1 John 2:7

John makes it clear he is *not* writing a new commandment. It is an *old* commandment and, yet, by the same token, new—not because of what it requires, but because of how it is achieved. What was not possible before has now been made possible through Jesus Christ. God's requirements have not changed—the *means of fulfilling the commandment* have been changed. To continue:

> Again, a new commandment I write to you, which thing is true in Him and in you, because the darkness is passing away [present tense], and the true light is already shining.
>
> verse 8

John makes his meaning clear in the next verses:

> He who says he is in the light, and hates his brother, is in darkness until now. He who loves his brother abides in the light, and there is no cause for stumbling in him. But he who

hates his brother is in darkness and walks in darkness, and does not know where he is going, because the darkness has blinded his eyes.

verses 9–11

What is the word we have had "from the beginning"? If you love your brother, you are in the light; if you hate your brother, you are in the darkness. This is the message all the way through the Scriptures. What could not be accomplished by the Law has been accomplished through the death of Jesus Christ by grace. Thus, it is an old commandment; but it is a new commandment. It is not new in its substance, but new in the way by which it is made possible.

In John's epistle we have a confirmation that he has in his mind the opening chapters of Genesis when he talks about "the beginning."

> For this is the message [or commandment] that you heard from the beginning [from Genesis], that we should love one another, not as Cain who was of the wicked one and murdered his brother. And why did he murder him? Because his works were evil and his brother's righteous. Do not marvel, my brethren, if the world hates you. We know that we have passed from death to life, because we love the brethren. He who does not love his brother abides in death.

1 John 3:11–14

The fact that John is referring to the first chapters of Genesis is evidenced by his reference to Cain and Abel. You will remember that the story of Cain and Abel presents two kinds of religion right at the source of human history. John draws from this story to present a contrast. Abel loved; Cain hated. Abel was in the light; Cain was in the dark. This is the message that was from the beginning and it was never intended to change. What *has* changed is the way by which we are able to fulfill this requirement.

Love Is . . .

The biblical meaning of *love* is mostly misunderstood. When the New Testament speaks of love, it is not primarily referring to feelings or outward symbols of affection. Somebody, using the Greek word for *love*, coined the phrase *sloppy agape*, which seems to typify too much of modern Christianity. It is indeed sloppy—emotional, insincere and frothy, containing no biblical reality. Love, as it is presented in the New Testament, is anything but *sloppy agape*. The Bible says, "Let us not love in word . . . but in deed and in truth" (1 John 3:18). This is a solemn thought, because Judas betrayed Jesus with the outward mark of love, which was a kiss.

If we go to the book of Ruth, we remember that Naomi had two daughters-in-law. Orpah kissed her, but Ruth stood by her. If I had to choose, I would rather have the one who stands by me rather than the one who kisses me. "Faithful are the wounds of a friend, but the kisses of an enemy are deceitful" (Proverbs 27:6). I would rather have a friend who tells me the truth even when it hurts, than an enemy who flatters me to my own downfall.

Love Is Expressed by Obedience

We have no right to talk of love for God unless we are willing to obey Him. The acid test of love is obedience. Obedience is the way that love is expressed; furthermore, it is the way that love is developed. The more we obey, the greater our love becomes.

Jesus says to His disciples, "If you love Me, keep My commandments" (John 14:15) and "He who has My commandments and keeps them, it is he who loves Me" (verse 21). Please notice: In order to keep His commandments, you must have them. This may sound simple, but it is important. In other words, you have an obligation to find out what His commandments are in order to keep them. Ignorance is no excuse, because we have a responsibility to discover them.

Our experience is somewhat like the little girl in a Christian family who was called to come for devotions. When her father called her she replied, "I'm not coming today."

Her father asked, "Why not?"

"Well," she said, "I already know more than I do!" In other words, the more she knew and did not do, the worse off she would be! Many of us are like that—we know more than we do. Jesus explains that it is not just knowing His commandments, it is keeping them:

> "He who has My commandments and keeps them, it is he who loves Me. And he who loves Me will be loved by My Father, and I will love him and manifest Myself to him." Judas (not

Iscariot) said to Him, "Lord, how is it that You will manifest Yourself to us, and not to the world?"

John 14:21–22

At this point one of Jesus' disciples asks Him an important question. Jesus has just told His disciples He is going to leave. The world will not see Him again, but then He says, "You will see me again." So Judas, puzzling over this statement, asks, "Lord, how is it that when You leave You are going to reveal Yourself to us but not to the world? What will be the difference? How will You do it?"

We Keep His Word

Jesus answers in the next verse, "If anyone loves Me, he will keep My word" (John 14:23). There is a difference between the world and the disciple of Jesus. The world does not keep the words of Jesus; the disciple *does*. It is through His word, kept by the disciples, that Jesus will reveal Himself to the disciples but not to the world. Then Jesus makes a wonderful promise to His disciples: "Jesus answered and said to him, 'If anyone loves Me, he will keep My word; and My Father will love him, and We will come to him and make Our home with him'" (John 14:23).

Can you imagine anything more wonderful? The Father and the Son will come and live with the one who keeps the words of Jesus. But please note: The issue is not merely knowing the words of Jesus. It is keeping them.

The apostle John repeats this same theme in his first epistle.

> Now by this we know that we know Him, if we keep His commandments. He who says, "I know Him," and does not keep His commandments, is a liar, and the truth is not in him. But whoever keeps His word, truly the love of God is perfected in him. By this we know that we are in Him.
>
> 1 John 2:3–5

One of the tests of whether or not we know God is whether or not we obey Him. This passage contains one of those many two-edged statements of the Bible. That is why we are told, "The word of God is . . . sharper than any two-edged sword" (Hebrews 4:12). John's statement, "Whoever keeps His word, truly the love of God is perfected in him," is two-edged. First, it means that perfect love is perfect obedience. But it also means that as we go on keeping His Word, His love is made perfect in us.

How do we increase in our love for God? I question whether or not the right thing to do is to sit in a church pew and pray for some kind of emotional experience. Love is not emotionalism. I would never suggest that you fast and pray to become loving, though I think there are matters for which we should fast and pray. But when you want to be loving, concentrate on obedience.

You will not develop love by continually thinking about how you feel. There is great danger in becoming introspective, analyzing yourself and pointing out all your faults. The longer you look into yourself, the worse you will feel in the end.

Self-criticism is not a Christian discipline; it is a humanistic discipline, and it is a practice in which Christians should never engage themselves. You are not spiritual because you feel condemned; when you feel condemnation you are unbelieving.

Preachers in particular need to come to the realization that it is not spiritual to make people feel guilty. For a period in my ministry I thought the more I made people feel guilty, the more powerful my messages were. I worked hard at making my congregation feel guilty and I achieved results. I roasted people, and they writhed and squirmed. The unfortunate result was that at the end of the message they would come up and say, "Wonderful message, Brother Prince! Wonderful!" But they never changed. They remained the same Sunday after Sunday. Finally, I thought to myself, *Something's wrong with this. I'm wasting my time.*

Eventually, the Lord showed me my problem. It is not God who makes people feel guilty; it is the devil. If we condemn people, we are doing the devil's work for him, and he does not even pay us! I found it is much more difficult to make people feel righteous than it is to make them feel guilty. But if we can help people experience the righteousness they have through faith in Christ, then we have succeeded in preaching the Gospel.

Now That We Know

We ended chapter four by presenting two questions:

1. What does God require of us?
2. How does God enable us to do what He requires?

In answer to the first question, it should be clear that "the righteous requirement" God expects is *love*, birthed in an attitude of obedience. In our next chapter, we will continue this exploration to find what, exactly, we must obey in order to have this kind of love.

6

What *Do* We Obey?

Now that we understand that love is both expressed and developed by obedience, we continue our exploration of God's righteous requirement by asking: *What, exactly, do we have to obey?*

Very simply, we are to obey *all that the New Testament teaches*. It would be convenient if I could give you a list of six things you could jot down as what Brother Prince says you have to do to be obedient. As we are about to learn, however, the Christian life is a journey of discovering all that the New Testament presents to us.

A dear friend of mine once decided to find out whether grace, as it is presented in the New Testament, really requires us to do anything; or if we can just go here and there by whatever feels good, drifting into or out of church whenever it suits us. Thus, he set out to see if the New Testament tells us to do specific actions. Some weeks later when I happened to stay in his home, he had read through 2 Peter and had already counted more than three hundred things the New Testament told him to do. God has set out for us in His Word all that He expects of us. It is our job to discover each of these requirements for ourselves.

At the same time, our understanding and application of God's Word will be continually unfolding and increasing. It is a journey; we will never know it all. Throughout history, one of the biggest mistakes of most religious groups is to believe they have come to the point where there is no more truth to discover and to know. If God brings a group into being as a spiritual movement to restore a certain truth to the Body of Christ and to accomplish a certain purpose, almost invariably, it seems that once they accomplish that task, the next thing they do is proclaim, "Now, that's all there is. There is no more." Then, because they are not open to receiving anything further, God must bring into being a different movement to bring further truth to the Church. Then, when He emphasizes that next truth, the main opponent of the new truth is almost always the previous group.

As the Church grows throughout history, it is like a building going up story by story, truth by truth. Whenever God wants another story added, He moves by the Holy Spirit, calls men and women into what He is doing, reveals truth to them, imparts power and grace and says, "Build the next story."

This group then builds the next story in a wonderful move of God and they say, "Now we'll put the roof on it!" But God never told them to put on a roof because He is planning to add another story. The next time the wind of the Holy Spirit blows, the first thing He has to do is blow off the roof! Then God must raise up a new group that is willing to go forward, and He commissions them to add the next story. Wise and gracious is the group that is able to say, "We don't have it all. Let's be open to what God will do next."

I have studied in some detail the history of the Pilgrims who initiated the spiritual life of the United States. One of the outstanding features of the Pilgrims was that they did not claim to know it all. That is why they called themselves "Pilgrims"; they understood they were on a journey. There was further truth ahead, and they needed to be open to it. There are few religious groups that have not said, "We can stop here. We've got it all." The Pilgrims deliberately did not do that. They challenged one another to go further, always with the qualification that wherever they went was substantiated by the Scriptures. I personally believe the immense progress and development of the American nation has been due to the spirit of openness out of which it was born.

The children of God in any nation set the spiritual tone for the whole nation. And, I believe it was the openness of the Pilgrims to further truth that made the United States probably the most open nation in human history to new ideas and development. Whenever the people of God in any nation put the roof on spiritual progress and say, "That's it!" they are cutting off the life of the nation.

Growing in Discernment

Paul addresses the need for continued growth in writing to the Philippians.

> And this I pray, that your love may abound still more and more in knowledge and all discernment, that you may approve the things that are excellent, that you may be sincere and without offense till the day of Christ, being filled with the fruits of righteousness which are by Jesus Christ, to the glory and praise of God.
>
> Philippians 1:9–11

Notice, Paul assumes that the Philippians have love because he knows them personally. Still, he tells them their love must increase more and more in the knowledge of God's will and in discernment. The Greek word translated in the New King James Version as "discernment" is the word that gives us the English word *aesthetic*; and a good translation would be *perceptive*. So Paul is saying, "It's good that you have love, but I want you to become better instructed and more perceptive." One of the traits I am continually learning (it seems too slowly) is that the key to progress in the Christian life is cultivating perceptivity to the Holy Spirit.

Paul tells the Philippians that their goal is to "approve all things that are excellent." A good marginal translation of this phrase is to "try the things that differ." One of the problems with most Christians today is they have very little spiritual perceptivity and cannot discern the difference between what is excellent and what is not. They will swallow anything as long as it is presented with a lot of fervor, accompanied by references to the Holy Spirit and an occasional Bible verse. As a Bible teacher who has devoted years to studying the Bible and trying to communicate its truth, I find that nothing discourages me more than when the same people who sat under my teaching and told me how much it benefited them listen to almost any strange teaching and declare how great it is.

God's will for us is to increase in knowledge and perceptivity so that we may know the difference between what is false and what is true, the self-exalting and the Christ-exalting, the soulish and the spiritual. If we do not learn these lessons, we will quickly be in trouble. Note again Paul's words:

> . . . that you may be sincere and without offense till the day of Christ, being filled with the fruits of righteousness which are by Jesus Christ, to the glory and praise of God.
>
> verses 10–11

In order to be sincere, without offense, and filled with the fruits of righteousness, we must increase continually in knowledge and perceptivity.

Paul applies this to himself by making it clear that he has not yet attained the goal. At the time he penned these words he had been in the ministry as an apostle several years, planted numerous churches, seen thousands of people converted and performed many miracles. Yet Paul says:

> Not that I have already attained, or am already perfected; but I press on, that I may lay hold of that for which Christ Jesus has also laid hold of me. Brethren, I do not count myself to

have apprehended; but one thing I do, forgetting those things which are behind and reaching forward to those things which are ahead, I press toward the goal for the prize of the upward call of God in Christ Jesus. Therefore let us, as many as are mature, have this mind; and if in anything you think otherwise, God will reveal even this to you. Nevertheless, to the degree that we have already attained, let us walk by the same rule, let us be of the same mind.

Philippians 3:12–16

If you notice there, Paul uses the word *perfect*, or *mature*, in two different senses, and there is an apparent conflict. In verse 12 he says, "Not as though I were already perfect [Greek: *mature*]." But, in verse 15 he says, "Let us, therefore, as many as are mature, have this mind." It is important to understand what Paul means here.

A good illustration is the growth of an apple. When an apple starts to grow on a tree it is a small, hard, green ball. It is certainly not a perfect apple—it is not mature, complete or ripe. Yet, it can be perfect for its stage of growth. In other words, there are no worms in it, no rottenness and no disease. Interestingly enough, if it does not go on growing to perfection, it will lose the perfection that it already has.

By way of application we can say that whatever stage of growth you are in, in that stage you can be perfect. There are no areas of unconfessed sin, no rebellion and no refusal to accept and obey God. You are perfect, but you are not perfect in maturity. If you do not press on to be perfect or mature, however, you will lose the perfection that you already have.

So Paul says, "I haven't arrived. I'm still pressing toward the mark. And, what I have learned I don't intend to give up." Never give up what you have learned. Proverbs 23:23 warns us: "Buy the truth, and do not sell it." You have to pay a price for the truth, so once you have bought it, never lose it. I never let go of any truth that I have learned from the Bible that works in my experience—I hold on to it! Even so, I bear in mind that what I have is not all there is to know. I walk in the light that I have, believing that the light will get brighter day by day.

Increasing in Knowledge

Consider how Paul expresses this in his letter to the Colossians:

> For this reason we also, since the day we heard it, do not cease to pray for you, and to ask that you may be filled with the knowledge of His will in all wisdom and spiritual understanding; that you may walk worthy of the Lord, fully pleasing Him, being fruitful in every good work and increasing in the knowledge of God; strengthened with all might, according to His glorious power, for all patience and longsuffering with joy; giving thanks to the Father who has qualified us to be partakers of the inheritance of the saints in the light.
>
> Colossians 1:9–12

What a beautiful statement! Do you realize that we can be filled with the knowledge of His will in all wisdom and spiritual understanding? Being filled with the knowledge of God's will is not an unattainable goal, because Paul never prayed for anything in the Holy Spirit that the Holy Spirit would not achieve. Let's consider this passage phrase by phrase.

"That you may walk worthy of the Lord, fully pleasing Him" (verse 10). Notice, you will not walk worthy of the Lord unless you are "filled with the knowledge of His will" (verse 9). This is a basic requirement of our Christian walk.

"Being fruitful in every good work and increasing in the knowledge of God" (verse 10). The knowledge of God must increase. We cannot be static; we must continue to grow.

"Strengthened with all might, according to His glorious power, for all patience and longsuffering with joy" (verse 11). These opening twelve verses of Colossians are "the inheritance of the saints in light" (verse 12). There is not one negative word or thought in those twelve verses. Everything is positive.

I would like us to notice how many *all*'s there are in these verses. Bear in mind that in the Greek language *all* and *every* are the same word.

> For this reason we also, since the day we heard it, do not cease to pray for you, and to ask that you may be filled with the knowledge of His will in *all* wisdom and spiritual understanding; that you may walk worthy of the Lord, fully [Greek: to *all* pleasing] pleasing Him, being fruitful in *every* good work and increasing in the knowledge of God; strengthened with *all* might, according to His glorious power, for *all* patience and longsuffering with joy.

Please take this opportunity to pause right here. Take a few minutes to read those few verses over and over until you begin to comprehend the standard God desires us to press toward.

Going forward now, let's look at Proverbs 4:18, which is one of my favorite Scriptures. It sums up this entire section succinctly: "But the path of the just is like the shining sun, that shines ever brighter unto the perfect day."

If you are walking in the pathway of the righteous, the light gets brighter on your path each day. And, any day you are walking in the previous day's light, you are moving backward. I do not say this to condemn anyone; I just wish to point out that every day has more light than the previous day—if we will receive it!

Love: Outpoured and Outworked

There is one more principle that we need to establish about love, which is profound. Love comes to us, or is developed within us, in two ways. There is the supernatural outpouring of God's total love, which can be given to us any time. But there is also the outworking of that outpoured love in our character and daily living, which is totally different. At some point God pours the whole of His love into our hearts with the Holy Spirit—in one act it is all within us!

I remember a psychiatrist who received the baptism with the Holy Spirit in an Assembly of God church where I was an associate pastor. He was not only a psychiatrist, but a stiff Presbyterian elder, as well. He had been seeking the baptism with the Holy Spirit for a long time and he came forward at the altar in our noisy Pentecostal church. A number of people were standing around him making a great deal of racket and laying hands on him. The entire experience must have been agony to the poor man's soul, but he was very desperate to receive the Holy Spirit.

After a little while they gave up, and my wife, Lydia, came forward and quietly laid hands on him. Almost immediately, he was baptized with the Holy Spirit and spoke in tongues. After a few moments, as he stood and turned around, the first person he saw was my wife. Quite spontaneously he threw his arms around her and embraced her. When I saw that, I said to myself, *When you see a psychiatrist who is a Presbyterian elder embracing a Pentecostal preacher's wife in an Assembly of God church, something real has happened!* At that moment he was filled with total love, and he simply had to embrace the first person he saw.

Now, it does not necessarily follow that he went home and was a perfect husband for the rest of his days. That is the outworking of God's love in our character and daily living. It is the relationship between that first outpouring of divine love and living it out in daily life that is our challenge.

Thankfully, however, we do receive an amazing outpouring of divine love: "Now hope does not disappoint, because the love of God has been poured out in our hearts by the Holy Spirit who was given to us" (Romans 5:5).

Paul does not say *some* of God's love, but *the* love of God has been poured out. "Poured out" is in the Greek perfect tense, meaning it is all there and we do not need any more. Asking for more love would be like someone standing beside Niagara Falls and praying, "Lord, I need water." God would have to answer, "Avail yourself of what you already have. You'll never need more than is already available." It is our job to take the power that is in that "Niagara Falls" of God's love and harness it in daily life. It requires hard work to avail ourselves of this power and see it begin to transform us, but it is the only path to maturity.

Daily Application

We read how this process is worked out practically in our daily lives:

> Grace and peace be multiplied to you in the knowledge of God and of Jesus our Lord, as His divine power has given to us all things that pertain to life and godliness, through the knowledge of Him who called us by glory and virtue, by which have been given to us exceedingly great and precious promises, that through these you may be partakers of the divine nature, having escaped the corruption that is in the world through lust. But also for this very reason, giving all diligence, add to your faith virtue, to virtue knowledge, to knowledge self-control, to self-control perseverance, to perseverance godliness, to godliness brotherly kindness, and to brotherly kindness love.
>
> 2 Peter 1:2–7

Let's consider this passage one verse at a time. First of all, please note that the Christian life is a life of multiplication. We can praise God for that! Grace and peace are multiplied to us in the knowledge of God and of Jesus our Lord, *"as His divine power has given to us all things that pertain to life and godliness"* (verse 3). Notice that God has already given us all things; there is nothing He has yet to give us. It has all been given us in Christ.

"Through the knowledge of Him who called us by glory and virtue" (verse 3). Everything is contained in the knowledge of Jesus Christ in whom are hidden all the treasures of wisdom and knowledge (see Colossians 2:3). Everything we are ever going to need for time and eternity is already ours in our knowledge of Jesus Christ.

"By which have been given to us exceedingly great and precious promises" (verse 4). Our inheritance is in the promises of God—everything is already there for us. A good illustration of how this works is given to us in the Old Testament. Under the old covenant, under a leader named Joshua (which is the same name as Jesus), God brought His people into a promised land. Under the New Covenant, under a leader named Jesus, God brings His people into a land of promises. The inheritance is in the promises. They were there for the people under Joshua and they are there for us. In the Promised Land was all that the people of Israel would ever need, just as all we will ever need is in the promises of God's Word.

Do you remember what God said to Joshua? "You've got to put your foot on every place to make it yours." Just as Joshua and Israel had to "put their feet" on the Promised Land to inherit it, we must "put our feet down" and stand on the promises God has given us in order to inherit His promises to us.

"That through these [the promises] *you may be partakers of the divine nature"* (verse 4). As you appropriate the

promises, you become a partaker of God's own nature. This is one of the most astonishing statements in the entire Bible.

"Having escaped the corruption that is in the world through lust" (verse 4). In the same proportion that you receive the nature of God, you will be delivered from the corruption that is in the world, because God's nature and corruption cannot occupy the same place. As you receive the nature of God through appropriating His promises in faith, you are delivered from the corruption that is in this world through the lust of evil, ungoverned, misdirected desire.

Then Peter goes on to say:

> But also for this very reason, giving all diligence [there is no place for laziness], add to your faith virtue, to virtue knowledge, to knowledge self-control, to self-control perseverance, to perseverance godliness, to godliness brotherly kindness, and to brotherly kindness love.
>
> verses 5–7

Peter here states that because we have received the nature of God, we must work out in our lives the character of God. It is one thing to have the divine nature; it is quite another thing to display the divine character. This is the focal point of Christian growth—transforming nature into character.

Here, then, are the seven stages of character growth as Peter has given them to us. The basic platform for the entire process is *faith*. We begin by faith because without faith it is impossible to please God. "For he who comes to God must believe that He is, and that He is a rewarder of those who diligently seek Him" (Hebrews 11:6). The basis of the whole life is faith in God, in Jesus Christ and in the Scriptures. To these we add:

1. Virtue (excellence)
2. Knowledge
3. Self-control
4. Perseverance (endurance)
5. Godliness
6. Brotherly kindness (love for fellow believers)
7. Love (divine love for all men)

These seven successive steps that follow from faith lead upward to the attainment of our goal. The first step we add to faith is *virtue*. The word *virtue* is not very familiar in modern English. I think the best English translation today is *excellence*, which rules out sloppiness and inefficiency.

When I was training young African teachers in Kenya, my primary aim was to lead them to Christ and to bring them into the baptism with the Holy Spirit. I discovered that when they professed faith in Christ, somehow they expected me to show them favor by judging their lessons more leniently. To their surprise I told them, "You're quite wrong. If you could be a teacher without Christ and the Holy Spirit, you should be twice as good a teacher with Christ and the Holy Spirit. I'm not going to judge you more leniently; I'm going to expect more of you."

Unfortunately, I find a similar attitude of laxity among many Western Christians. No matter what your profession is, whether you are a teacher, a janitor, an attorney, a bus driver, a business professional or a homemaker, when you come to Christ, the next thing you must add to your character is excellence.

To excellence we add *knowledge*; the knowledge of God's will, which is in His Word.

To knowledge we add *self-control*. You cannot successfully run the race of faith without self-control. If you indulge every mood, every whim, every fancy and every appetite, you will never be an overcomer. Paul compares the Christian life to people striving for success in athletic games (see 2 Timothy 2:5). He says that everyone who strives to succeed in the games exercises self-control in everything. If you have ever considered the life of champion athletes, you will note that they are careful about the hours they sleep, the food they eat, the company they keep and the exercise they take. Their whole lives are directed toward jumping a little higher, running a little faster or diving a little better than somebody else. Paul states that if you are going to be a successful Christian you have to cultivate self-control just as much as those athletes. Self-control is right in the middle of this list; I believe it is the ingredient around which everything turns.

Then we go to *perseverance*, or endurance. Perseverance is holding out against adversity, opposition and misunderstanding. The first mark of an apostle is perseverance. "Truly the signs of an apostle were accomplished among you," Paul says, "with all perseverance, in signs and wonders and mighty deeds" (2 Corinthians 12:12). The first mark of a true apostle is not signs and wonders; it is the character mark of perseverance. The apostle holds on when everybody else turns back. That is endurance.

After perseverance comes *godliness*. Godliness is a word rarely used in contemporary society, most probably because there are not many people to whom it could be applied. But the fact remains that God Himself esteems and requires godliness in His people. I would define *godliness* as "a life that would be meaningless if there were no God." Or perhaps it is "a life that is a continual reminder to all of the reality of God." Do you know somebody whose life is like that—perhaps a godly, praying mother or father or pastor? You only have to speak to them or be in the same room with them and you are reminded of God.

Paul gives a beautiful description of that kind of effect: "But thanks be to God, who always leads us in triumphal procession in Christ and through us spreads everywhere the fragrance of the knowledge of him" (2 Corinthians 2:14, NIV). Fragrance is a beautiful but elusive thing. The human nose is so sensitive. Someone wearing a fragrance of some kind may walk past you and your nose will pick up something in the air that no scientific instrument can detect. That person left something behind, something beautiful and something that stimulates thoughts or memories.

We are to communicate Christ's victory to all with whom we have contact. Out of this life of victory something lovely develops. Everywhere we go, we spread the fragrance of the knowledge of Jesus and an awareness of the godliness that comes as a result of walking close to Him.

Beyond godliness is *brotherly love*. Do you really love your fellow believer? Believe me, genuinely loving other believers takes some doing. Then, when you can honestly say, "I've arrived—I love my fellow Christians," God says, "No, you have one more step."

The final step is *agape*, divine love. Divine love is loving the people who do not love you—your enemies and your persecutors. *Agape* gives and gives and asks for nothing back. It continually blesses and gives out. *Agape* is the climax of the development of Christian character. I want you to see that this kind of love is built on a solid foundation of progressing character. It is not an accident; it is not a whim; it is not a feeling; and it is not a spiritual gift. It is an achievement. If you do not work at it, you will not achieve it.

Working Out Righteousness

As we mature in the daily outworking of love, we also need to grow in the area of righteousness. The two work together: God requires a righteousness that is expressed by divine love worked out in our daily lives. Just as love is both a gift and something that must be worked out, so is righteousness. We must make the effort to move from *imputed* righteousness (the gift we receive from God) to *imparted* righteousness (the way we live). Let's look at these facets of righteousness a little more closely.

Imputed Righteousness

When you receive Jesus Christ by faith as your Savior, you are clothed by divine grace with His righteousness. Isaiah says the Lord gave him a garment of salvation and a robe of righteousness (see Isaiah 61:10). When you receive the garment of salvation, God next gives you a robe of spotless righteousness. This robe is Christ's righteousness credited to you. "[God] made Him who knew no sin to be sin for us, that we might become the righteousness of God in Him" (2 Corinthians 5:21). This is imputed righteousness. God credits it to your account on the basis of what Christ has done.

Paul uses Abraham as an example of imputed righteousness, quoting Genesis 15:6: "[Abraham] believed in the LORD, and He accounted it to him for righteousness." Abraham's faith was accounted (reckoned or imputed) to him for righteousness. Paul goes on to say that Abraham is the pattern for us, and righteousness will be imputed to us also if we have faith:

> And therefore "it was accounted to him [Abraham] for righteousness." Now it was not written for his [Abraham's] sake alone that it was imputed to him, but also for us. It shall be imputed to us who believe in Him who raised up Jesus our Lord from the dead.
>
> Romans 4:22–24

If we believe in the death, burial and resurrection of Jesus on our behalf, His righteousness is imputed to us the moment we believe. There is no more guilt, no more condemnation, and the devil has nothing to say against us any longer.

But for you to become a mature Christian, that imputed righteousness must be worked out in your daily living as part of your character. This is imparted righteousness—the way you live.

Imparted Righteousness

The challenge of maturing as a Christian is transferring imputed righteousness to imparted, outworked righteousness. Unfortunately, for most people, that is a lengthy and sometimes difficult process!

One of the clearest statements in Scripture of the relationship between the gift and outworking of righteousness is found in Philippians:

> Therefore, my beloved, as you have always obeyed, not as in my presence only, but now much more in my absence, work out your own salvation with fear and trembling; for it is God who works in you both to will and to do for His good pleasure.
>
> Philippians 2:12–13

As Paul explains here, *God works in and we work out.* If God did not work His righteousness in us, we would have nothing to work out. Notice that not only does God work in "to do," but He also works in "to will." He puts in us *the will* to do that which is right.

Being a Christian should not be a continual struggle to do something you do not want to do. If you are continually struggling to do what you do not want to do, then you have never been born again; because when you are born again you receive a natural desire to do the will of God. God works in you "to will" and then "to do," but God works *in you* only in proportion as *you work out.* If you stop working "out," God can no longer work "in," because there is something in your heart like a traffic jam. In a traffic jam the car behind

113

you cannot move into the place you occupy until you move forward. Some Christians have been parked in one place and the meter time expired a long while ago! God says, "I'm waiting. I'd like to do a lot more for you, but until you do what you already know to do, how can I give you any more?" Work out what God works in—that is what it means to transfer imputed righteousness to imparted righteousness.

Making Ourselves Ready

As a conclusion to this topic, we will look at this glorious Scripture:

> "Let us be glad and rejoice and give Him glory, for the marriage of the Lamb has come, and His wife has made herself ready." And to her it was granted to be arrayed in fine linen, clean and bright, for the fine linen is the righteous acts of the saints.
>
> Revelation 19:7–8

The great climax of all ages is the marriage of the Lamb. The Bride of the Lamb is the Church, the Body of Christ. But notice, the Bride must make herself ready. Have you ever been in the preparation for a marriage where the bridegroom came and got the bride ready? Nowhere! The bride works hard at her dress, her hair, her fingernails—everything must be perfect. If ever there is a time when a young woman is busy, it is when she is getting ready for her marriage. Today the Church needs to be busy preparing for her marriage to the Lamb.

The fine linen that makes up the Bride's wedding dress is the righteous acts of the saints. This is the outworked righteousness of the saints. All your life long you are spinning the fabric for your wedding garment. Every righteous act you make is another thread.

Lydia and I had a fellow missionary friend in Palestine who became ill and was told she was going to die. Being a believer, she was prepared to die. One night the Lord gave her a vivid dream. In her dream she was sewing a beautiful white garment and as she looked closely at it, she saw there was a great deal of the garment still missing. Through this dream the Lord showed her that she had not finished her life's work. Ultimately, she did not die; the Lord raised her up to complete her work.

Many times I have pondered the message of that dream. All through our lives as Christians we are working on our wedding garments. The linen we are weaving into this garment is our outworked righteousness as saints. Considering this, I have often suspected that if some Christians do not change their manner of life, all they will have for a wedding garment is a miniskirt! Certainly not heaven's appropriate fashion for weddings.

We understand, then, that God requires from us, as outworked righteousness of the Law, just one word: *love.* All the Law is fulfilled in that one word. This answers the question: *What does God require of us?* We now turn to the second question: *How does God enable us to do what He requires?* To address this question, we must understand *how grace operates*, which is the topic of the next chapter.

7

Grace: God's Enablement

How does God enable us to do what He requires? Just as the first question of what God requires was answered by the single word *love,* the second question is also answered by a single word: *grace.* We will begin our examination of how God enables us by explaining how grace operates in us. This equips us to see the love of God developed within us. I believe the operation of grace is one of the most difficult spiritual truths for the natural mind to grasp. The remainder of this book will be devoted to exploring this beautiful and profound theme.

Grace Defined

Let's begin with a definition of *grace.* This definition is accepted by many Bible scholars, but certainly does not exhaust the full meaning: *Grace is the free, unmerited favor of God toward the undeserving and the ill-deserving.*

Notice, first of all, that grace is *free.* Grace cannot be earned; it cannot be worked for. Also, please notice that grace is not only toward those who are undeserving but even to those who are *ill-deserving.* In other words, even when we deserve judgment and wrath, God, out of His grace, offers us good. The word *favor* is an alternative word for *grace.* Especially in the Old Testament, both words are used almost interchangeably.

Grace is one of the key concepts of the whole Bible. The unfolding of grace begins in the Old Testament and is brought to completeness with the revelation of Jesus Christ in the New Testament. In the New Testament, the Greek word for *grace* occurs 155 times, mainly in the epistles.

The normal New Testament salutation among Christians was "Grace and peace. . . ." Sometimes they added "mercy" and said, "Grace, mercy and peace. . . ." It is implied by this salutation that if you want peace, you must have grace first. The only way we can have true peace is out of the grace of God.

Almost all New Testament epistles (or letters) begin and end with *grace.* Their salutation is usually something like "Grace and peace be to you"; and most of them end with "the grace of God be with you," "the grace of the Lord Jesus Christ be with you" or simply "grace be with you." This is significant because the epistles essentially deal with working out the truth of the Gospel in daily living. The manner in which these letters open and close makes it clear that in

118

order to work out the truth of the Gospel, we must begin and end with the grace of God. If we do not start and finish with God's grace, Christian living is not possible on the level that the New Testament outlines.

Let's look briefly at the original words for *grace* used in the Greek of the New Testament and in the Hebrew of the Old Testament.

The Greek word for *grace* is *charis*. This word also appears in another form in the word *charisma*. *Charisma* is the word that is used for the gifts of the Holy Spirit and for various other manifestations. *Charisma* means "grace made manifest or made specific." *Charis* is "grace, in general"; *charisma* is the specific manifestation of that grace in someone's life.

The Beauty of Grace

Two Hebrew words are commonly used in the Old Testament: *chen* and *ratson*. They are used more or less interchangeably. *Chen* means "beauty" and *ratson* means "pleasure." It can mean both "favor" and "beauty." The basic meaning of these words in both languages is "beauty or attractiveness."

We need to bear in mind that grace is always beautiful and it is always attractive. A person who is in the grace of God is an attractive person. A congregation in which the grace of God rests is an attractive congregation. If a congregation does not have the grace of God working in its midst, it may have the truth but it will not attract anyone. It takes the grace of God to attract people to the truth. It says about the early Church in Jerusalem that "great grace was upon them all" (Acts 4:33) and "the Lord added to the church daily" (Acts 2:47). What attracted people to the early Church was the manifestation of the grace of God in His people. The beauty of the Lord, the attractiveness of God, was upon them.

One common phrase in the Old Testament incorporating the word *chen* is to "find grace [or favor] in the eyes" of somebody. Genesis 6:8 says that "Noah found grace [or favor] in the eyes of the Lord." The favor Noah found in God's eyes distinguished Noah from all the other men of his generation; and, because of Noah, his family also found grace in the eyes of the Lord.

Grace has something to do with the way we look at people. And, in the context of this study, the grace of God is about the way God looks at us. There is a saying that goes, "Beauty is in the eyes of the beholder." This little phrase contains a good deal of truth. I have noticed that one man may look at a certain woman and think she is beautiful while another man might not give her a second glance. They are looking at exactly the same person, but it is the way that the man looks at the woman that determines what he sees in her.

The Source of Grace

Applying this truth as we examine the grace of God, we find that it begins not with us but with God. God's grace originates out of the way He chooses to look upon us. When He looks upon us with favor, then grace begins to operate in our lives. The idea that grace depends primarily on the way God looks at us is beautifully illustrated by the Levitical blessing. This blessing is shared between Christians and Jews alike.

> And the LORD spoke to Moses, saying: "Speak to Aaron and his sons, saying, 'This is the way you shall bless the children of Israel. Say to them:
>
> > "The LORD bless you and keep you;
> > The LORD make His face shine upon you,
> > And be gracious to you;
> > The LORD lift up His countenance upon you,
> > And give you peace."'"
>
> Numbers 6:22–26

There are six parts to this blessing.

First, "the Lord bless you."

Second, "the Lord keep you."

Third, "the Lord make His face shine upon you."

Fourth, "and be gracious to you."

Fifth, "the Lord turn His face toward you" (literal Hebrew reading).

And, sixth, "give you peace."

Notice that the phrase *the Lord be gracious to you* is both preceded and followed by the mention of the Lord's face. First, the Lord makes His face shine upon His people, and then the Lord turns His face toward them. The operation of the Lord's grace depends on the way He looks at us. The last part of the blessing is, "And give you peace." Once again, real peace only comes out of the operation of the grace of God.

Grace in Times of Need

There is a beautiful example of the Lord's grace manifested by His looking on His people in the second chapter of Exodus. The end of this chapter describes Israel's misery in Egypt and how the Lord began to show grace and favor toward them:

> During that long period, the king of Egypt died. The Israelites groaned in their slavery and cried out, and their cry for help because of their slavery went up to God. God heard their groaning and he remembered his covenant with Abraham, with Isaac and with Jacob. So God looked on the Israelites and was concerned about them.
>
> Exodus 2:23–25, NIV

The Israelites are in desperate need and misery, unable to help themselves; all they can hope for is the grace of God. God hears their groaning and responds: "God looked on the Israelites and was concerned about them." God's favor began to operate when He turned His face toward the Israelites in concern for them. Then, in a practical way, He began to move on their behalf to intervene and deliver them. The point where "God looked on the Israelites" was the point at which His grace began to operate.

Another wonderful verse reaffirms the truth that God is the only source of true grace: "But may the God of all grace, who called us to His eternal glory by Christ Jesus, after you have suffered a while, perfect, establish, strengthen, and settle you" (1 Peter 5:10).

God is the God of *all* grace. In other words, grace comes solely and entirely from God; there is no other source of grace in the universe. If you want grace, you must go to God. His grace is the only force in the universe that matures us and makes us firm, strong and steadfast. This is the favor of God as His face is turned toward us.

Our Need for Grace

At the beginning of this chapter we defined grace as *the free, unmerited favor of God toward the undeserving and the ill-deserving.* To appreciate the full measure of God's grace let's consider the last half of this definition—the *undeserving* and the *ill-deserving.* These words refer to the condition of the human race left to itself apart from God. Once we understand how desperate the human spiritual state really is, we understand why grace alone can meet our needs.

A People in Darkness

A picture of humanity apart from God's grace is found in Matthew's gospel. This passage describes the beginning of the earthly ministry of Jesus in Galilee with a quote from the Old Testament, Isaiah 9:1–2:

> Now when Jesus heard that John had been put in prison, He departed to Galilee. And leaving Nazareth, He came and dwelt in Capernaum, which is by the sea, in the regions of Zebulun

and Naphtali, that it might be fulfilled which was spoken by Isaiah the prophet, saying:

> "The land of Zebulun and the land of Naphtali,
> By the way of the sea, beyond the Jordan,
> Galilee of the Gentiles:
> The people who sat in darkness have seen a great
>   light,
> And upon those who sat in the region and shadow of
>   death
> Light has dawned."
>
> Matthew 4:12–16

The picture given to us of humanity when Jesus comes on the scene is of a people living in darkness and in the land of the shadow of death. Their condition may be summed up in three phrases: *darkness, hopelessness* and *no expectation but death*. This is the condition of humanity apart from the grace of God. Notice Isaiah says that they *sat* in the land of the shadow of death. They were motionless, they had no way to move; therefore, they could not escape and had no alternatives. Each day the long, dark shadow of death fell a little more extensively across their lives. There was nothing they could do but wait hopelessly. It is a picture of complete and desperate hopelessness.

Spiritually Dead

In the New Testament Paul describes the spiritual condition of humankind apart from grace:

And you He made alive, who were dead in trespasses and sins, in which you once walked according to the course of this world, according to the prince of the power of the air, the spirit who now works in the sons of disobedience, among whom also we all once conducted ourselves in the lusts of our flesh, fulfilling the desires of the flesh and of the mind, and were by nature children of wrath, just as the others. But God, who is rich in mercy, because of His great love with which He loved us, even when we were dead in trespasses, made us alive together with Christ (by grace you have been saved).

Ephesians 2:1–5

Apart from God we were spiritually dead in our transgressions and sins. We were cut off from the life of God and incapable of responding to God in any way. Consider the helplessness and the hopelessness of a dead person. You may present the Law to a dead person, but he cannot read it. You may preach sermons to a dead person, but he cannot hear them. You may set good examples for a dead person, but he cannot see your deeds. There is nothing that will help a dead person, and the helplessness of death describes our condition before God. By nature we were cut off from God, incapable of helping ourselves, incapable of responding, incapable of doing any good things. We were very simply—dead!

Being dead in sin is the primary reason that the Law cannot help us spiritually: "For if there had been a law given which could have given life, truly righteousness would have been by the law" (Galatians 3:21). If a law could give life, then a law could help a dead person. But the Law cannot give life because it is not in the nature of law to impart life. The

Law tells us what to do—it is beautiful, holy and just—but it cannot give us life. The primary need of a dead person is life, and life comes solely by grace.

Living at a Distance from God

King David speaks about the condition of the human race in general, referring to us as the children of men:

> The LORD looks down from heaven upon the children of men, to see if there are any who understand, who seek God. They have all turned aside, they have together become corrupt; there is none who does good, no, not one.
>
> Psalm 14:2–3

David says that as God looks down from heaven on humanity, He is looking for anyone who has done anything good or even anyone who has sought out God because of his or her need. He cannot find a single person who did good or sought for Him. Apart from the grace of God we cannot even see our own need for God. We are like dead people who are incapable of seeing the desperate situation in which we exist. There is nothing we can do for ourselves until God's grace comes into operation.

Immediately after I came to know the Lord Jesus Christ and tasted of His grace in a personal way, I would have said this about myself: "I was a sinner, there is no doubt about that. But there was something good in me—I had a real desire for the truth. All my life I had been pursuing the truth even to the point of becoming a professional philosopher."

I genuinely believed that God worked through this little bit of good in me to bring me to Himself. Out of Scripture and through the Holy Spirit, however, I eventually saw that even my desire for the truth was not in me by nature, but had been placed there by God's grace. His grace had begun working in me as a teenager even though I did not come to know the Lord in a personal way until I was in my mid-twenties.

God's grace works in our lives long before we know we need it and even before we are willing to turn to Him. We are in darkness; we are dead, incapable of helping ourselves, incapable of responding and incapable of doing anything good. Charles Wesley, in his hymn, "And Can It Be?" expresses eloquently the human condition and the work of grace in freeing us from darkness and death.

> Long my imprisoned spirit lay,
> Fast bound in sin and nature's night.
> Thine eye diffused a quickening ray;
> I woke; the dungeon flamed with light.
> My chains fell off, my heart was free,
> I rose, went forth, and followed Thee.

Grace through the Cross

As we move deeper into the mystery of God's grace, we need to understand that grace can only come into operation as a result of the atoning death of Jesus Christ on the cross. If Christ had not died on the cross as our substitute and as our sin offering, there would have been no possibility for grace to operate in our lives.

> For what the law could not do in that it was weak through the flesh, God did by sending His own Son in the likeness of sinful flesh, on account of sin: He condemned sin in the flesh, that the righteous requirement of the law might be fulfilled in us.
>
> Romans 8:3–4

God had to deal with sin through the cross before we could be reckoned righteous by His grace. The atonement of Christ did five specific things that made a way for the grace of God to begin to operate in our lives. The work of the cross is not limited to these five things, but these are especially important as far as the release of God's grace toward us.

1. Christ Paid the Penalty for All Sins

Speaking about the redemption that is in Christ Jesus, Paul writes this: "God set forth [Christ Jesus] as a propitiation by His blood, through faith, to demonstrate His righteousness, because in His forbearance God had passed over the sins that were previously committed" (Romans 3:25).

Jesus, on the cross, paid the due penalty for all past sinful acts. In His forbearance, God had passed over these sinful acts of many preceding generations without bringing final judgment. He was looking forward to the time when all judgments would be settled once and for all by the death of Jesus Christ.

The Greek word for *propitiation* is the same word that is used in the Greek version of the Old Testament for the *mercy seat,* which was the covering of the Ark of the Covenant. On the mercy seat was sprinkled the blood of the sin offering, which made atonement for the sins of the people. This is a powerful picture, because the Ten Commandments were inside the Ark representing the requirements of the Law. Those Commandments had been flouted and broken. But Jesus, by His propitiation on the cross, became the mercy seat that once and for all covered the broken Law.

It was a sin punishable by death for anybody to lift the mercy seat and look inside the Ark (see Numbers 4:20; 1 Samuel 6:19). In other words, once the broken Law has been dealt with, we are never to go back and look at it again because it is covered by the mercy seat, the propitiation of Jesus Christ on the cross. The question of our past sins has once and for all been dealt with by the death of Jesus. The devil can never bring up against us anything that we have committed in the past *if it has been confessed* and if we have claimed the forgiveness of God through the atonement of Jesus Christ. Never let the devil accuse you about the past!

2. Christ Terminated the Law As a Means of Righteousness

Jesus, by His death on the cross, terminated the Law of Moses as a means of righteousness. This truth was covered in detail in chapter 1, so we will only mention it here. Romans 10:4 says: "For Christ is the end of the law for righteousness to everyone who believes."

If you are a believer, then Christ ended the Law for you as a means of righteousness. Whether you are Jew or Gentile makes no difference. Christ did this for any and all believers.

3. Christ Settled Satan's Claims Against Us

The death of Christ settled Satan's claims against us, and thus delivered us from the devil's dominion. We read this truth in Colossians:

> Giving thanks to the Father who has qualified us to be partakers of the inheritance of the saints in the light. He has delivered us from the power of darkness and conveyed us into the kingdom of the Son of His love.
>
> Colossians 1:12–13

The word *power*, which is the Greek word *exousia*, is usually translated "authority." Christ, therefore, delivered us from the *authority* of darkness. Satan has authority over the rebellious because, as the prince of the power of the air, he is the spirit that works in the children of disobedience (see Ephesians 2:2). Darkness has authority over the children of darkness. When we are in rebellion against God, we are under the authority of Satan. But through the death of Jesus Christ on the cross, God has delivered us from the authority of darkness and translated us into the Kingdom of the Son of His love.

I prefer the word *translated* for the word *conveyed*, which is used in this version. There were two persons in the Old Testament who were translated: Enoch and Elijah. Both of them went completely, leaving nothing behind. We have been totally translated from one kingdom to another; not partially, it is not a process. Our total being—spirit, soul and body—has been moved out of the realm of the authority of Satan into the Kingdom of Jesus Christ. Because of what God did through Christ on the cross, Satan has no more dominion over us and no more claims against us.

In the verses that follow, Paul summarizes these first three points:

> And you, being dead in your trespasses and the uncircumcision of your flesh, He has made alive together with Him, having forgiven you all trespasses, having wiped out the handwriting of requirements that was against us, which was contrary to us. And He has taken it out of the way, having nailed it to the cross. Having disarmed principalities and powers, He made a public spectacle of them, triumphing over them in it.
>
> Colossians 2:13–15

First, point one, Paul states that God has forgiven us all our trespasses (verse 13). All our wrong acts that we have ever committed, God has forgiven us through the death of Christ.

Then, point two, he writes that God has blotted out the handwriting of ordinances that was against us, which is the Law (verse 14). The Law was contrary to us because every time we tried to get to God, the Law stood in the way by reminding us that we were transgressors who had no right of access to God. But God, through the death of Christ, moved the Law out of the way, nailing it with Christ to the cross. That ended the Law as a means of righteousness.

Point three (verse 15) says that through the death of Christ, God has disarmed the principalities and powers of Satan. Satan's dominating power has been stripped of all its authority and all its claims over us.

There is a logical order here. First of all, the past must be dealt with by all our past sinful acts being forgiven. Secondly, the Law must be taken out of the way so that it is no longer against us because we are not under it. Then, on the basis of those two facts, we are free from Satan's dominion over us.

If any past sinful acts were still reckoned against us, or if we were still required to keep the Law, then we would not be free from the dominion of Satan. Only when you are absolutely convinced that all your past sins are forgiven once and for all, and that you are no longer required to be made righteous by the keeping of the Law, only then can you be free from the dominion of Satan. As long as Satan can keep you in any way guilty, either because of unforgiven past sin or because you are trying to live up to a standard that you believe God requires of you—then Satan has dominion over you.

As far as the Christian is concerned, Satan's basic activity is to function as the accuser of the brethren. If we are ever to walk in victory, we must come to the place where we rebuff his accusations, denying their power against us. Only when we are totally free of guilt are we a match for Satan. His supreme objective is to keep Christians feeling guilty.

Unfortunately the devil has been greatly assisted over the centuries by our churches. Historically, the average church operates in a way that keeps you feeling at least slightly guilty.

Most of the hymns we have sung over the centuries have been sin-centered hymns, and most sermons are designed to make us feel guilty by pointing out how far short we fall. I believe most churchgoers feel holiest when they feel guilty; in fact, they would think it was presumptuous not to feel guilty.

It has been my observation that people go through all the ceremonies of the church and repeat all the items of the creed, but they do not genuinely believe them. If they did believe what they said in the creeds, they would act differently.

Every major section of the Body of Christ basically believes the same principles: We were helpless, hopeless, hell-deserving sinners, but God in His infinite grace and mercy gave His Son that all our sins can be forgiven and that we might be reckoned entirely righteous. Even so, we go through the same confessions Sunday morning after Sunday morning, yet walk out of church looking as though nothing important has really happened.

As I have meditated on this tendency, I have sometimes pictured a respectable religious lady attending her church on a Sunday morning. Having confessed all these great truths in the creed and having sung them in the hymns, she walks out of the service as prim and proper as when she walked in. Leaving the church she drops her beautiful lace handkerchief. A little boy scampers up to her, picks up the handkerchief and says, "Ma'am, here's your handkerchief." Suddenly, her face brightens with joy. She is much more excited about getting her handkerchief back than she is about having her sins forgiven! One thing is real to her, the other one is not. Her church participation is just theology and creeds—but it has no meaning in her daily experience.

Religious people think it is a little fanatical when exuberant Christians jump up and down and dance. But this is the only logical way to act if we really believe what we say we believe. Anything else is inconsistent and ridiculous. The only way we are able to be free from the dominion of Satan is to become fully convinced of the reality of our forgiveness and our freedom from the Law.

4. Christ Put Away Sin

The fourth accomplishment of Jesus through His death on the cross was *to put away sin*. I pointed out in chapter 2 that our problems in this life are the result of two forces working together within us. The first is the *force of sin*, which is a deceitful, corrupt, destructive spiritual power at work in the universe. The second is the *old carnal nature*, which the New Testament calls "the old man." This is the nature within us that is prone to rebellion. When the force of sin works on the old man, the result is sinful living. We have these two elements in the problem, both of which must be dealt with by the death of Christ on the cross.

In dealing with these two forces, therefore, Christ first put away sin. In the ninth chapter of Hebrews the writer points out that Christ had to offer only one sacrifice since He was not like the Old Testament priests who needed to keep offering the same sacrifices over and over again. Christ had to do it only once; His was one sufficient, complete sacrifice that never had to be repeated. Thus, the writer says:

> He then would have had to suffer often since the foundation of the world [if He had been an Old Testament priest]; but now, once at the end of the ages, He has appeared to put away sin by the sacrifice of Himself.
>
> Hebrews 9:26

When Jesus died on the cross He became the sin offering promised in Isaiah 53:10: "When You make His soul an offering for sin, He shall see His seed, He shall prolong His days, and the pleasure of the LORD shall prosper in His hand." On the cross Jesus exhausted the sin of the world in His own soul. When He died, sin was put away by His sacrifice once and for all. As we go beyond the cross, we enter into a realm where sin has no access. Sin has no power, because it has been put out of operation.

5. Christ Executed Our Carnal Nature

Then, in dealing with the second of these two forces mentioned above, we see that in the death of Christ our carnal nature, our old man, was executed or put to death: "Knowing this, that our old man was crucified with Him, that the body of sin might be done away with, that we should no longer be slaves of sin" (Romans 6:6).

The Greek text uses the simple past tense: *was crucified*. This tense is used to describe a single historical event that happened once and was never repeated. Our old man was crucified in Jesus Christ. When Jesus died on the cross, my old nature died in Him as a single event that never needs to be repeated. That ended it. Here is my version of this verse, which I have amplified for clarity:

> Our old man was crucified with Him, that the body of sin—
> that is, the sinful rebellious nature in me—might be put out of
> operation that, henceforth, we should not be the slaves of sin.

I prefer to say, "put out of operation," instead of "done away with." Why? Because the old nature is not totally eliminated, but it is put out of operation so that it no longer has any power. The only way to escape from the slavery of sin is through the death of the old man. As long as the old man lives, he lives as the slave of sin.

God has only one program for the old man. He does not send him to church, teach him the Golden Rule or ask him to memorize Scripture. God's only program for the old man is to execute him! This is all that God can do for him. But the problem is that most Christians do not know this simple truth.

Paul says, "*Knowing* this, that our old man was crucified." Then he adds, "Likewise . . . reckon yourselves" (Romans 6:11). In other words, believe what God says. God said it; you believe it. If God says you are dead, then you must reckon yourself dead. Accept this simple truth and agree with what God says about your old nature. This is God's program for dealing with the old man.

Grace could not have come into operation unless these five accomplishments had taken place through the death of

Christ. The work of the cross once and for all removed every barrier to the free flow of the grace of God into the entire world. The cross is the basic requirement that sets the grace of God in operation.

Having established the basis for the operation of grace through the cross, we will further understand the operation of grace by making two clear biblical distinctions in the next two chapters: first, the distinction between grace and the operation of the Law as it was expressed under the Old Covenant; then, the distinction between grace and works, which is a major theme of the New Testament.

8

Two Distinctions:
New and Old Covenants

If we can understand the distinction between the way grace operates and the way the Law operates, we ultimately will eliminate a great deal of confusion in our lives. As we are learning, many believers struggle constantly because they do not understand the difference and try to walk in a mixture of grace and law. I want to begin this section of the study with a simple summation of the difference between grace and law: *Law commands the "old man" from without. Grace writes upon the heart of the "new man" within.*

Essentially, law is external; it is outside of me. I look objectively at the Law and I say, "That's what I have to do." Grace, however, is internal. It does something inside me that results ultimately in my acting in accordance with what has been written on my heart.

Paul gives us a summation of the difference between law and grace, and points out seven ways in which grace differs from the Law. I believe this is one of the clearest and most succinct statements of this distinction in the entire New Testament. I want to quote this passage here for you to read it in its entirety. Then we will consider it in detail.

> Do we begin again to commend ourselves? Or do we need, as some others, epistles of commendation to you or letters of commendation from you? You are our epistle written in our hearts, known and read by all men; clearly you are an epistle of Christ, ministered by us, written not with ink but by the Spirit of the living God, not on tablets of stone but on tablets of flesh, that is, of the heart. And we have such trust through Christ toward God. Not that we are sufficient of ourselves to think of anything as being from ourselves, but our sufficiency is from God, who also made us sufficient as ministers of the new covenant, not of the letter but of the Spirit; for the letter kills, but the Spirit gives life. But if the ministry of death, written and engraved on stones, was glorious, so that the children of Israel could not look steadily at the face of Moses because of the glory of his countenance, which glory was passing away, how will the ministry of the Spirit not be more glorious? For if the ministry of condemnation had glory, the ministry of righteousness exceeds much more in glory. For even what was made glorious had no glory in this respect, because of the glory that excels. For if what is passing away was glorious, what remains is much more glorious.

Therefore, since we have such hope, we use great boldness of speech—unlike Moses, who put a veil over his face so that the children of Israel could not look steadily at the end of what was passing away.

2 Corinthians 3:1–13

It will help us understand Paul's approach to the subject of the New Covenant in this passage if we understand the context in which he wrote these words. Paul's authority had evidently been challenged by some in Corinth. That is why he raises the question, "Do you Christians in Corinth not already know me? Do I need some special letter of recommendation introducing me to you?"

In verse 3 he writes, "Clearly you are an epistle of Christ, ministered by us." In essence, he is saying, "You are the only letter of recommendation that I need." This is one of the most challenging statements I have found in the New Testament. In effect, Paul declares to the ancient world, "If you want to know what I believe, go to Corinth and you'll find out. Look at the people. They're my letter; they're my theology."

This continually challenges me as a Christian leader. As a pastor or teacher of the Scriptures, I should be able to say to the world, "Do you want to know what I believe? Look at my congregation. They are the demonstration of what I believe." If what I teach and preach does not work out in people's lives, then why bother with it?

If the Gospel could work in Corinth, which was one of the most wicked, dissolute cities of the ancient world, it should be able to work in New York, Tokyo or Moscow. In the first chapter of John's gospel he writes, "The Word was made flesh" (John 1:14, KJV). In his first epistle, he adds that we have heard Him, we have seen Him, our hands have handled Him (see 1 John 1:1, KJV). The life that was in Jesus was manifested in a way that all the world could see. And God's purpose for the Church is precisely the same: that the Word of God be made flesh in us. It is His intent that we demonstrate the Gospel collectively, as a body, to the world. Anything less is failure. The world should be able to see, handle and hear God in us.

The Glory of the New Covenant

Following his initial statement, Paul goes on to explain how this life came to be manifested in the church in Corinth. This glorious life had been brought into the church by the presence of the Spirit of God—not by the Law of Moses. In fact, there had been synagogues in most of the great cities of the ancient world for hundreds of years, but their presence had no impact on those cities. The Law had been there and been taught Sabbath after Sabbath, but it had changed nothing.

Paul then makes seven points of distinction between the operation of the grace of the New Covenant and the operation of the Law of the Old Covenant. I have summarized these seven points in the table below for ease of reference as we consider each in more detail.

Operation of Grace vs. Operation of Law
from 2 Corinthians 3:3–13

Verse	Law (Old Covenant)	Grace (New Covenant)
3	Ink	Holy Spirit
3	*External* tablets of stone	*Internal* tablets of the heart
6	Letter	Spirit
6–8	Death	Life
9	Condemnation	Righteousness
10–11	Temporal glory	Continuing glory
12–13	Veiled meaning	Plainness of speech

Writings and Tablets

Verse 3 contains the first two sets of distinctions: "Clearly you are an epistle of Christ, ministered by us, written not with ink but by the Spirit of the living God, not on tablets of stone but on tablets of flesh, that is, of the heart."

Law writes with *ink on external tablets;* grace writes with the *Holy Spirit on the heart.* This simple statement is the very essence of the distinction between the Law and grace. The Law is outside of you, written on tablets of stone. The Law says, "Do this! Don't do that! And if you do that, you'll be punished." When you look at the Law, you say to yourself, "I mustn't do this; I must do that." The tragic result, as we have seen, is that you end up doing the exact opposite of what you decided to do. Why? Because inside you is an uncrucified rebel, and the more this rebel is confronted with the Law, the more rebellious he becomes.

As we saw in chapter 2, the Law actually stirs up and strengthens sin (see 1 Corinthians 15:56; Romans 6:14). Thus, God says, "I'll put the rebel to death, create a new nature in you and then by My Spirit I'll write on the heart of the new man inside him." This is the operation of grace.

Letter and Spirit; Death and Life

This is the next set of distinctions:

Who also made us sufficient as ministers of the new covenant, not of the letter but of the Spirit; for the letter kills, but the Spirit gives life. But if the ministry of death, written and engraved on stones, was glorious, so that the children of Israel could not look steadily at the face of Moses because of the glory of his countenance, which glory was passing away, how will the ministry of the Spirit not be more glorious?

2 Corinthians 3:6–8

Paul says that as a minister of the New Covenant, he does not write in *letters* engraved on stones, but by the *Holy Spirit* he writes spiritual truth on the hearts of believers. Why? Because the *letter kills* but the *spirit gives life*. The Law, Paul says, is a minister of *death*. Whenever the Law is applied, it results in *death*. But wherever grace is given, it produces *life*.

It is breathtaking to consider the number of funerals that took place in the Exodus. Moses led 600,000 able-bodied men of war out of Egypt. Forty years later, only two of them, Joshua and Caleb, entered the Promised Land. That tells us that 600,000 men, and presumably about the same number of women, had died, meaning approximately 1,200,000 people died in forty years. Thirty thousand people died each year, or about eighty funerals per day! This happened because the people agreed to keep the Law and then ended up breaking it.

An aspect of the Law we do not readily understand or see so easily is that its fruit is death. Plain and simple, the Law brings death. Only the Spirit brings life.

Condemnation and Righteousness

Verse 9 tells us: "If the ministry of condemnation had glory, the ministry of righteousness exceeds much more in glory."

The Law brings *condemnation*, but grace brings *righteousness*. Some people are perplexed when I tell them that it is the devil who makes them feel guilty, because we are not accustomed to thinking of the devil as the source of our guilt. Much of our religious training has taught us to believe that when we feel guilty we are being very pious. As a result we do not feel right unless we feel guilty.

We must remember that it is the devil and the Law that minister condemnation and guilt. The New Covenant, which is grace, ministers righteousness. It is not our goal to make people feel guilty. It is our goal through the Gospel to assure people that they have been made righteous through the work of Christ.

The Concept of Glory

Let's continue now with verses 10–11: "For even what was made glorious had no glory in this respect, because of the glory that excels. For if what is passing away was glorious, what remains is much more glorious." (See also Exodus 34:29–35.)

In these two verses Paul is referring to the time when Moses came down from the mountain after communing with God for forty days and nights while receiving the Law. After being in God's presence, his face shown so gloriously that his fellow Israelites were afraid to come near him. In order not to scare them, Moses put a veil over his face and talked with them from under a veil. But, Paul says, this glory, as great as it was, was a superficial, *temporal glory* that eventually faded from Moses' face.

The temporal glory of the Law is a very significant concept. Wherever you encounter a legalistic religious system, it has a certain superficial glory. These systems have pomp, ceremony, vestments, organs, choirs and a whole array of attributes that impress the soulish man—but all these are only *temporal and impermanent.*

Growing up, I spent hours in some of the most famous religious buildings of Britain. The chapel of King's College, where most of my professional academic career occurred, is probably one of the most famous religious buildings in the world. Over the years I spent many hours in this beautiful building. I enjoyed the lovely music of its world-renowned choir and admired the stunning architecture with the carved woodwork and the ornate stained-glass windows. I had to acknowledge I felt a certain glory. But I would walk out and ten minutes later feel as cold as death. The temporal glory never lasts. It is fading; it is transient.

We must learn to see the difference between the superficial, soulish, impermanent glory of man-made religion and the true inward spiritual, *abiding glory* of the Gospel. The Gospel brings a *permanent glory*, but it is spiritual. The soulish man cannot appreciate the spiritual glory of the Gospel. Religious people cannot enjoy the liberty of the Holy Spirit, because one is soulish, the other is spiritual. This is why Jesus says, "And no one, having drunk old wine, immediately desires new; for he says, 'The old is better'" (Luke 5:39). If you are accustomed to the glory of legalism, you will not immediately want to embrace the glory of the freedom of the Gospel. You can be so "intoxicated" by the glory of the old that you will not desire the glory of the new.

Veiled Meanings or Open Language

Finally, Paul outlines the seventh point of distinction:

Therefore, since we have such hope, we use great boldness of speech—unlike Moses, who put a veil over his face so that the children of Israel could not look steadily at the end of what was passing away.

2 Corinthians 3:12–13

Paul says that a veil still remains on the hearts of the Jewish people (see 2 Corinthians 3:15). They cannot see that the meaning and purpose of the Law was to point them to the Messiah. They see its superficial glory but they do not

147

see that its glory is finished. The Law is *veiled* as far as its true purpose and meaning extend. It does not come out and speak the truth clearly, but the Gospel does. That is why Paul can say that he uses great boldness, or plainness, of speech.

I am convinced the Holy Spirit honors plain, bold speech. He is the Spirit of truth and He blesses us when we "tell it like it is." I have become increasingly suspicious of truths that must be explained in allegories and illustrations. I believe teaching in types and shadows may have a valid place, but it can never be a basis for establishing doctrine. Doctrine is established from the clear, simple statements of the New Testament.

I love to go back and study the historical patterns of the sacrifices and the feasts of the Law. They are a picture of the truth of the Gospel. But they only illustrate the truth; they can never establish it.

Two More Important Differences

Beyond these seven distinctions, there are two more important ways in which the New Covenant differs from the Old Covenant. They are pointed out in this passage from Hebrews, which is actually a quotation of Jeremiah 31:31–34:

> For if that first covenant had been faultless, then no place would have been sought for a second. Because finding fault with them, He says: "Behold, the days are coming, says the LORD, when I will make a new covenant with the house of Israel

and with the house of Judah—not according to the covenant that I made with their fathers in the day when I took them by the hand to lead them out of the land of Egypt; because they did not continue in My covenant, and I disregarded them, says the LORD. For this is the covenant that I will make with the house of Israel after those days, says the LORD: I will put My laws in their mind and write them on their hearts; and I will be their God, and they shall be My people. None of them shall teach his neighbor, and none his brother, saying, 'Know the LORD,' for all shall know Me, from the least of them to the greatest of them. For I will be merciful to their unrighteousness, and their sins and their lawless deeds I will remember no more."

Hebrews 8:7–12

To review, as we saw in 2 Corinthians 3:3, the Holy Spirit writes the laws of God not on tablets of stone as something outside us that we have to try to keep, but rather in our hearts and minds where they are naturally expressed in the things that we do.

Proverbs 4:23 tells us: "Keep your heart with all diligence, for out of it spring the issues of life." What you have in your heart will determine the way you live, and when God's laws are written in your heart you will live God's way.

The Holy Spirit writes those laws that God wants us to keep. And as we saw in chapter 3, those laws have never changed throughout human history. God's requirement has always been the same: first, love for God, and second, love for our neighbor.

No Mediator Needed

The writer of Hebrews then goes on to point out two more distinct differences between the Old and New Covenants. The first difference is that every believer knows God in a direct and personal way without the need of a mediator: "All shall know Me, from the least of them to the greatest of them" (Hebrews 8:11).

A mediator actually comes between people and brings them into contact with each other. Paul tells us that the Old Covenant required a mediator between God and man:

> What purpose then does the law serve? It was added because of transgressions, till the Seed should come to whom the promise was made; and it was appointed through angels by the hand of a mediator. Now a mediator does not mediate for one only, but God is one.
>
> Galatians 3:19–20

The Law was not given directly to Israel by God; it was given by angels to Moses, who was the mediator between heaven and earth.

Under the New Covenant people do not need to be taught how to know the Lord, because as God Himself says: "All shall know Me, from the least of them to the greatest of them." When you meet Jesus Christ, you meet God. In John 17:3, Jesus says: "And this is eternal life, that they may know You, the only true God, and Jesus Christ whom You have sent." The New Covenant gives us each a direct, personal relationship with God through Jesus Christ without any need for a mediator.

No More Offerings

The second distinct difference between the Old and New Covenants is that there is no more consciousness of sin by God, and, therefore, no more offerings for sin are required: "For I will be merciful to their unrighteousness, and their sins and their lawless deeds I will remember no more" (Hebrews 8:12).

The very memory of our sin has been blotted out from God's consciousness. The writer emphasizes this again two chapters later:

> For by one offering He has perfected forever those who are being sanctified. But the Holy Spirit also witnesses to us; for after He had said before, "This is the covenant that I will make with them after those days, says the LORD: I will put My laws into their hearts, and in their minds I will write them," then He adds, "*Their sins and their lawless deeds I will remember no more.*" Now where there is remission of these, there is no longer an offering for sin.
>
> Hebrews 10:14–18 (emphasis added)

If our sins have been forgotten by God, we are not going to need another sin offering, and we have no need to continually remind God of our past sin. Whereas the Old Covenant required many sacrifices, which were a continual reminder of sins, there has been one final, sufficient sin offering and there are no more sin offerings required.

From the New Testament we have seen nine distinct ways in which the operation of grace differs from the operation of law as it is expressed in the Old Covenant.

151

The Law writes with ink. Grace writes with the Holy Spirit.

The Law writes on external tablets of stone or other material. Grace writes on the internal tablets of the heart of the renewed believer.

The Law writes letters. Grace writes spiritual truth.

The Law ministers death. Grace ministers life.

The Law ministers condemnation. Grace ministers righteousness.

The Law has a temporary glory. Grace has an abiding and exceeding glory.

The Law uses veiled meanings. Grace uses free, open language.

The Law was given through a mediator. Grace gives us a direct, personal relationship with God through Christ.

The Law reminds us of our sin through continual sacrifices. Grace removes our sin from God's consciousness by one complete, sufficient sacrifice.

We have seen how grace differs from law by comparing the Old and New Covenants. Before we look further into the nature of grace we need to make one more clear distinction, which is how grace differs from works. This is a major theme of the New Testament, which we will consider in the next chapter.

9

Two Distinctions:
Grace and Works

In the last chapter we looked at the ways in which grace and law operate and summarized them as follows: *Law commands the "old man" from without. Grace writes upon the heart of the "new man" within.*

Now we focus on another important distinction that Scripture makes, the *distinction between grace and works*. There is both an intellectual aspect and a spiritual aspect to this truth. If we are willing to apply our minds, we can gain an intellectual appreciation out of which will come spiritual enrichment. But we need to use our intellect to understand these distinctions that the New Testament so carefully makes.

Probably the key passage for this distinction between grace and works is Ephesians 2:8–9: "For by grace you have been saved through faith, and that not of yourselves; it is the gift of God, not of works, lest anyone should boast."

Here Paul makes two positive statements and one negative statement about grace and works. The two positive statements are: *by grace . . . through faith.* Grace and faith must always be kept together because grace always comes through faith. Then Paul makes the negative statement: *not of works.* Grace always excludes works. We cannot work for grace and we cannot deserve it. We must receive grace by faith. Grace and works are contrasted all through the New Testament; they are two mutually exclusive alternatives.

Paul affirms this in his letter to the Romans: "And if by grace, then it is no longer of works; otherwise grace is no longer grace. But if it is of works, it is no longer grace; otherwise work is no longer work" (Romans 11:6). In other words, if you can earn something, then it cannot come by grace. And the opposite is also true: If something comes by grace, you cannot earn it.

The contrast between grace and works points us to the two mutually exclusive routes to achieve righteousness with God that we have observed. One path is through keeping the Law; the other path is through Christ. The Law demands works; but Christ offers grace. We must choose one path or the other, but we cannot have a little of one and a little of the other. This is brought out in the passage that speaks of Jesus as the eternal Word of God made flesh: "For the law was given through Moses, but grace and truth came through Jesus Christ" (John 1:17).

In addition, as we have learned, to be justified or to achieve righteousness by the Law, we have to observe the *whole law all the time*. The Law, given through Moses, was a single comprehensive system presented at one time. Moses continually warned the Israelites not to add to it or take away from it. It is a complete indivisible unit. (See Deuteronomy 4:2; 12:32.)

In Galatians 3:10, Paul expresses the same truth:

> For as many as are of the works of the law are under the curse; for it is written, "Cursed is everyone who does not continue in all things which are written in the book of the law, to do them."

Paul is quoting from Deuteronomy 27:26, where Israel is agreeing to keep the Law. Notice also, if you wish to rely on achieving righteousness by keeping the Law and you break it at any one point, you come under the curse that the Law itself pronounces. Israel could not come under the Law without accepting that curse upon themselves. This is a very sobering thought when we think of trying to achieve righteousness by any form of law.

The Law Brings the Knowledge of Sin

No person has ever succeeded in keeping the whole law all the time—the single exception being Jesus Himself. Paul says, "Therefore by the deeds [works] of the law no flesh [no human being] will be justified in His sight, for by the law is the knowledge of sin" (Romans 3:20).

155

In the New Testament "works" are always associated with keeping the Law as a means of righteousness, whereas "faith" is always the means by which we obtain the righteousness that is by grace. The Law can never give us righteousness, but as we saw in chapter 3, the Law does give us something very important—the knowledge of sin. In this passage where Paul says, "the law" the article *the* has been inserted by the translators. This could also be translated simply, *law*. It would then read, "By the deeds of law no flesh will be justified in His sight."

First and foremost, this verse applies to the Law of Moses, but it also applies to every other kind of law. This means no one will ever be justified in the sight of God by keeping religious laws or church rules. This is important. Most Protestant believers like to think they are not under the Law of Moses, but then we make our own little laws by which we measure righteousness. Every denomination has its own laws—whether Baptist, charismatic or Catholic. No religious law, however, will ever cause anybody to be reckoned as righteous in the sight of God.

The main issue in the New Testament is whether we are made righteous by keeping laws or by faith. Through my Christian experience and ministry, I have rarely encountered people who have given any serious consideration to this critical question. Rather, they have switched from the Law of Moses, which was a perfect law given by God, and made their own sets of laws. The result is legalism.

The Problem of Legalism

I believe legalism is the greatest single problem of the Christian church. Legalism is, first of all, *the attempt to achieve righteousness with God by keeping a set of rules*. If you are attempting to be righteous with God by any set of rules, you are under legalism. There is nothing wrong with having rules. We need them. It is wrong, however, to believe that keeping those rules will make us righteous with God.

Legalism is the cause of much of the sin in the church. Many sincere and honest Christians have embraced a set of "do not" rules such as: Do not look at another woman. Do not drink alcohol. Do not wear certain articles of clothing. Do not go to the movies. Do not associate with particular people. They think that observing these prohibitions will make them righteous. When our attention is focused on such regulations, however, we become enslaved by them. The way to be pure is not to focus on resisting lust, because the more you focus on lust, the more it dominates your thinking. There is a totally different way of becoming righteous. It is a righteousness from God, which is by faith in Jesus Christ.

If the Law is ruled out as a means of righteousness, the only way to be in God's favor is through Christ. Paul goes on to say this:

> But now the righteousness of God apart from the law is revealed, being witnessed by the Law and the Prophets, even the righteousness of God, through faith in Jesus Christ, to all and on all who believe. For there is no difference; for all have

sinned and fall short of the glory of God, being justified freely
by His grace through the redemption that is in Christ Jesus.

Romans 3:21–24

Please notice, first of all, that righteousness comes "through
faith." True righteousness is given us "by His grace" with
no distinction between Jew and Gentile, between Catholic
and Protestant, or between one nationality and another. Paul
is very clear that we are all alike in one point—we all have
sinned and fall short of the glory of God. Since we cannot be
justified by the works of the Law, therefore, we must accept
the only alternative, which is God's grace. We cannot earn
it. We must receive it by believing in Christ Jesus.

Abraham and Faith

Paul's letter to the Romans deals extensively with the questions of grace (or faith) and works. At the heart of his argu-
ment is the fourth chapter, where he looks to two of the great
fathers of Israel—Abraham and David. He proves from the
Old Testament Scriptures that each of them was not justified
by works but by faith. He focuses mainly on Abraham, who
is the father of all who believe.

> What then shall we say that Abraham our father has found
> according to the flesh? For if Abraham was justified by works,
> he has something to boast about, but not before God. For
> what does the Scripture say? "Abraham believed God, and it
> was accounted to him for righteousness." Now to him who

158

works, the wages are not counted as grace but as debt. But to him who does not work but believes on Him who justifies the ungodly, his faith is accounted for righteousness.

Romans 4:1–5

Paul opens this chapter with an important question for both Jews and Gentiles. How did Abraham achieve righteousness with God? Paul contends that Abraham achieved righteousness by faith, and he quotes one of the most important passages from the Old Testament, Genesis 15:6. At this point in the narrative, Abraham is childless and God is giving him the promise of a natural child from his own body, even though he and Sarah are both well past the age of having children.

Then He [the Lord] brought him [Abraham] outside and said, "Look now toward heaven, and count the stars if you are able to number them." And He said to him, "So shall your descendants be." And he [Abraham] believed in the LORD, and He accounted it to him for righteousness.

Genesis 15:5–6

Abraham at that point did absolutely nothing but believe. Paul then points out that this act of faith was how Abraham achieved righteousness. He did not earn it. It was not on the basis of what he had done. Rather, it was credited to his faith alone. Then Paul makes the application to all believers:

Now to him who works, the wages are not counted as grace but as debt. But to him who does not work but believes on

Him who justifies the ungodly, his faith is accounted for righteousness.

Romans 4:4–5

This is one of the most powerful verses in the New Testament because it confirms that the one designated way to receive righteousness from God is the same way Abraham received it. The first thing you must do is to stop doing anything: "To him who does not work." You must come to the end of all that you can do to earn God's favor so that you have nothing to do but believe. This is the pattern and example of Abraham.

In verses 6–8, Paul refers to King David:

Just as David also describes the blessedness of the man to whom God imputes righteousness apart from works: "Blessed are those whose lawless deeds are forgiven, and whose sins are covered; blessed is the man to whom the LORD shall not impute sin."

Paul is quoting from Psalm 32:1–2, where David says there are three things included in this blessing. First, our lawless deeds have been forgiven; second, our sins have been covered; and third, God no longer takes our sin into account. This beautifully expresses the negative side of reckoning righteousness to us. On the positive side, God reckons righteousness to us; and on the negative side, He is no longer reckoning our sins against us. This blessing comes "apart from works"—by faith alone. We are never saved by faith *plus* something else. The only condition for being a spiritual descendant of Abraham is faith.

Abraham, Our Pattern

It is important to understand that Abraham is more than just an example. He is a pattern. He went ahead and laid out the pathway of faith by taking certain steps. And, if we truly are to be his descendants, we must walk in the same pathway following in his steps. Paul points this out:

> And he [Abraham] received the sign of circumcision . . . that he might be the father of all those who believe, though they are uncircumcised, that righteousness might be imputed to them also, and the father of circumcision to those who not only are of the circumcision, but who also walk in the steps of the faith which our father Abraham had while still uncircumcised.
>
> Romans 4:11–12

I believe there are five steps on the pathway of faith that our father Abraham took in seeing God's promise fulfilled:

First, he accepted God's promise, without asking for any evidence.

Second, he recognized that, by himself, he was incapable of producing what the Lord had promised.

Third, he focused without wavering on the promise, and this was reckoned to him as righteousness.

Fourth, God intervened. Both Abraham and Sarah received supernatural life in their bodies.

Fifth, the promise was fulfilled and God was glorified.

This is the pathway of faith that is set before every one of us. It is not an external ordinance written in stone. Rather, it is a lifelong walk of faith following in the footsteps of Abraham. We must accept God's promises just the way they are; we must admit we are incapable of producing what God has promised in our lives; and we must focus on the promise and not on our own ability or inability. Then we will receive the supernatural grace and power of God released in our lives through our faith, and the result will bring glory to God.

Jesus Christ, Our Way

Certainly Abraham is our father in the faith, our pattern for walking the pathway of faith. Now we turn to our Savior, Jesus Christ, who has provided the way for us to attain true righteousness in the sight of God. Romans 10:4 sums up the relationship between Christ and the Law as a means to righteousness: "For Christ is the end of the law for righteousness to everyone who believes."

Once you believe in Christ, you may no longer pursue the Law as a means to achieving righteousness with God. The Law is still a part of the eternal Word of God; it is a marvelous demonstration of God's justice and God's standards. It is also a part of the total culture and history of God's people, Israel. In these ways, Christ has not abolished the Law. *But when Christ died on the cross, He once, for all time, ended the Law as an acceptable means for achieving righteousness with God.* We have, therefore, no other alternative—it is grace or nothing.

Grace vs. Justice

There is one more important distinction that also arises out of the study of grace, which is the distinction between grace and justice. God's nature could be compared to the two sides of a coin. These two sides are summed up in Isaiah 45:21, where the Lord is speaking through the prophet: "And there is no other God besides Me, a just God and a Savior."

On one side of the coin, justice; on the other side of the coin, God presents Himself as a Savior. Justice corresponds to the Law and demands works. The Savior side of God corresponds to grace and requires faith.

Contemporary society is tremendously confused about justice. There is a sloppy, sentimental idea of justice that excuses as many criminals as possible while providing little justice for the victims. This is not true justice, which is very exact and impartial. Real justice does two things: It rewards and protects the righteous; and it punishes the sinner and the lawbreaker. Like the two sides of God Himself, justice has those two sides, and we cannot eliminate either side and retain justice.

Absolute Standards

God's justice is an absolute standard: "I will make justice the measuring line, and righteousness the plummet" (Isaiah 28:17).

Isaiah uses two metaphors taken from building construction. Every builder is familiar with the measuring line, or ruler, and the plummet, or plumb line. The ruler measures the length and the plumb line determines whether a wall is truly vertical or tilted. If the architect says the width of a wall must be six inches, and the ruler shows that the wall is five and seven-eighths inches wide, it does not pass inspection.

The same absolute standard holds true if we consider the plumb line. If we need to know that a certain wall is vertical, we hang the plumb line down the side. If it is one-sixteenth of an inch away from the base of the wall, we know that the wall is not vertical. It does not matter whether the wall is one-sixteenth of an inch or two inches away from vertical. The fact remains: The wall is not vertical.

By comparing His justice to a measuring line and a plumb line, God makes it clear that His justice is not only unvarying, but also impartial. God's justice measures all exactly the same whether they are Jew or Gentile, Protestant or Catholic, religious or atheist. God does not have different standards of justice. People may think that because they are much closer to matching a man-made set of rules than others that they are somehow better off. Unless they are *exactly* the right measurement, however, which is keeping the whole of the Law all of the time, it does not matter whether they are close or far away. *They are not accepted.*

God measures every person with the same ruler and checks every life with the same plumb line. In His justice there is no element of mercy.

The exactness and the severity of justice is summed up in this passage from Leviticus, which is a part of the legal code given by God to Moses:

> "Whoever kills any man shall surely be put to death. Whoever kills an animal shall make it good, animal for animal. If

a man causes disfigurement of his neighbor, as he has done, so shall it be done to him—fracture for fracture, eye for eye, tooth for tooth; as he has caused disfigurement of a man, so shall it be done to him."

Leviticus 24:17–20

This is justice; there are no alternatives. Justice is the objective, unvarying ruler and plumb line that hangs down against every life. Many people in the world today are demanding justice—often on understandable grounds, because of incidents of political, racial or religious oppression. In our relationship with God, however, we do not want to ask for justice. We need mercy!

When I consider people asking for justice I often think of the story about a woman who went to the photographer to have a portrait taken. In due course, she went back to see the proofs. When the photographer handed her the proofs she looked at them and did not like what she saw! She turned to the photographer and said, "These don't do me justice."

The photographer looked at her for a moment and replied, "Lady, you don't need justice. You need mercy!" The same is true for each of us: We don't need justice; we need mercy! If we ask for justice, we may get it. But we may be sorry we got it when it comes!

Two Sides to the Coin

God's justice is only one side of the coin, however. He is also the Savior. He is "My God of mercy" (Psalm 59:17). The

165

source of grace is the same as the source of justice. We may only obtain grace from the same source that dispenses justice.

To understand why this is so, consider the following example. Let's suppose you have been found guilty of a criminal offense. On the appointed day you appear in the courtroom and the judge is about to pass sentence upon you. Of course, you are very nervous, so you have your lawyer with you to represent you and your family and friends are present to give support. First, you turn to your lawyer and say, "Oh, I really would like to be pardoned. I really need mercy."

"Well," your lawyer answers, "I've done my best. But now it's in the judge's hands."

You turn to your relatives and you say, "I really need mercy!"

They reply, "We want you to have mercy, but we can't do anything about it. It's up to the judge."

You turn to your friends and say the same thing, but they shrug their shoulders and point to the judge. The only one who can pardon is the judge. The one who administers justice is the one who can also offer grace. Because God is the final source of justice for all humankind, He is also the only source of all grace for all men and women everywhere for all time.

In this chapter we have considered the distinction between grace and works. The contrast between grace and works points us to the two mutually exclusive routes to achieve righteousness with God. One path is through keeping the Law. The other path is through Christ. The Law demands works; but Christ offers grace. We must choose one path or the other. We cannot have both.

In the next chapter we want to begin examining the ways in which the Scriptures declare we can obtain the grace of God in our daily lives.

10

Receiving Grace

We have defined grace as *the free, unmerited favor of God toward the undeserving and the ill-deserving.* We have also seen that the Law demands works, but that Christ offers us grace—something that we cannot earn, that we do not work for, but which we may receive by faith. The key question then becomes: *How do we receive the grace of God?*

God Gives Grace to the Humble

Before we address this question directly, we must consider one essential requirement for receiving God's grace, which is *humbling ourselves.* We must come to grips with the fact that humility is a decision we must make for ourselves. No one else can do it for us. I do not believe it is fully scriptural to pray, "God, make me humble." I believe the Scripture clearly teaches that if we wish to become humble, we must humble ourselves.

To confirm this, we will look at several passages from the New Testament. Here is the first: "He gives more grace. Therefore He says: 'God resists the proud, but gives grace to the humble.' Therefore submit to God. Resist the devil and he will flee from you" (James 4:6–7).

James is quoting from Proverbs 3:34, which points out that there are two different attitudes God holds toward humankind. To the proud God offers opposition; but to the humble He offers grace. We are, therefore, to "submit to God." In other words, if you want God's grace, you must lay aside pride and submit yourself to Him. Then, and only then, we may "resist the devil" knowing he will flee from us. Once we have submitted to God, then we are in a position to resist the devil. If you try to resist the devil without being submitted to God it can be disastrous!

The New Testament also instructs us to humble ourselves toward one another. Peter quotes the same Old Testament passage that James referenced, and he writes:

> Likewise you younger people, submit yourselves to your elders. Yes, all of you be submissive to one another, and be clothed with humility, for "God resists the proud, but gives grace to the humble." Therefore humble yourselves under the mighty hand of God, that He may exalt you in due time.
>
> 1 Peter 5:5–6

Peter, like James, states that we must humble ourselves under God's mighty hand. But he also says we must "be clothed with humility" toward one another. God requires that we humble ourselves toward Him and that we also humble ourselves toward our fellow believers. I believe humbling ourselves toward one another is the true test of whether or not we have truly humbled ourselves before God.

The essence of humbling ourselves is *acknowledging that we need God's grace.* God never thrusts His grace on those who do not see their need of it. There is a beautiful pattern of humility in the song of praise that the virgin Mary gave to the Lord after the angel had announced that she was to become the mother of the Messiah, the Son of God. This beautiful song is known as the Magnificat, from the Latin word for "praise" or "glorifying."

> And Mary said:
> "My soul magnifies the Lord,
> And my spirit has rejoiced in God my Savior.
> For He has regarded the lowly state of His
>   maidservant;
> For behold, henceforth all generations will call me
>   blessed."
>
> Luke 1:46–48

Please notice what it was that caused the Lord to pick Mary for this unique honor among all women. It was her "lowly," or humble, state. When the angel first appeared and addressed her, he said to her, "Rejoice, highly favored one" (verse 28).

Favored is the same Greek word as *grace*. The high grace of God was bestowed upon Mary because of her humble state.

Then Mary's song continues:

> "For He who is mighty has done great things for me,
> And holy is His name.
> And His mercy is on those who fear Him
> From generation to generation.
> He has shown strength with His arm;
> He has scattered the proud in the imagination of their
>   hearts.
> He has put down the mighty from their thrones,
> And exalted the lowly.
> He has filled the hungry with good things,
> And the rich He has sent away empty."
>
> verses 49–53

The emphasis of this passage is again on the humble and the hungry, those who feel their need of God. On the other hand, God rejects the proud and the rich, those who are sufficient in themselves—those who, in their own eyes, need nothing from God.

Those Who Need God

The barrier of pride that keeps God's grace out of the lives of so many often takes the form of *self-righteousness*. Jesus taught about the danger of self-righteousness and how it keeps the grace of God out of our lives. He taught this in the parable of the Pharisee and the tax collector:

Also He spoke this parable to some who trusted in themselves that they were righteous, and despised others: "Two men went up to the temple to pray, one a Pharisee and the other a tax collector. The Pharisee stood and prayed thus with himself, 'God, I thank You that I am not like other men—extortioners, unjust, adulterers, or even as this tax collector. I fast twice a week; I give tithes of all that I possess.' And the tax collector, standing afar off, would not so much as raise his eyes to heaven, but beat his breast, saying, 'God, be merciful to me a sinner!'"

Luke 18:9–13

At the beginning, Jesus identifies the problem as trusting in our own righteousness. Notice that the prayer of the Pharisee was totally centered on himself and how righteous he was. This is contrasted with the tax collector who humbly asked for God's mercy. The Greek says, "God, have mercy on me, *the* sinner." In other words, the tax collector recognized that he was the one who needed mercy. He did not look around at anybody else. He did not compare himself with others. He merely looked to God. In fact, he would not even lift his eyes physically toward God; but inwardly he considered God's righteousness, His holiness and His justice. He said, "God, I'm the sinner. I'm not parading my righteousness or my goodness. I'm the one in need."

In concluding the parable, this is Jesus' comment: "I tell you, this man went down to his house justified rather than the other; for everyone who exalts himself will be humbled, and he who humbles himself will be exalted" (verse 14).

Again, the key to receiving grace and mercy is humbling ourselves. The religious self-righteousness of the Pharisee kept him from receiving grace. He was so self-occupied with his own righteousness, with all the good things he was doing and how much better he was than others, that the barrier of self-righteousness excluded the grace of God from his life. The tax collector had no such barrier. He just opened up and received the grace of God. In the end it was the tax collector who was justified, or acquitted. He was accepted by God.

It is the clear testimony of Scripture that the one essential requirement for receiving God's grace is *humbling ourselves*. It is a decision that each of us must make and an attitude we must continually cultivate. Once we have humbled ourselves, we are ready to receive the grace of God.

How to Receive God's Grace

The ability to receive God's grace is of vital importance for each of us. There are two aspects to this transaction. The first is negative and the second is positive.

1. Stop Working

The negative aspect may be summed up in two simple words that are very surprising to most people: *Stop working*. You must stop trying to earn God's approval. As long as you are trying to earn the grace of God you cannot receive it. God cannot give you His grace on the basis of what you do because that would be a false basis. If God gave grace to you based on what you did, you would have a false picture of yourself, of God and of everything that is involved in His relationship with us.

This first requirement, which is very difficult for religious people, is absolute and God will not change it. Paul states:

> Now to him who works, the wages are not counted as grace but as debt. But to him who does not work but believes on Him who justifies the ungodly, his faith is accounted for righteousness.
>
> Romans 4:4–5

Notice the vitally important words: *To him who does not work.* Then, once you stop working, you must simply trust God, who justifies the ungodly. This, of course, is humbling because it means you are putting yourself in the category of those who need to be justified because they are ungodly. This is the part that is very, very difficult for religious people to see. They cannot conceive of themselves as being categorized with the ungodly.

To the one who trusts God, who justifies the ungodly, his faith is credited as righteousness. From this point forward you are living on God's credit; you are no longer living on the produce of your own labor. This is God's grace, because your faith is credited to you as righteousness. You are not considered righteous because of what you have done, but because you believe in God who justifies the unrighteous. This is the negative aspect of receiving God's grace. *We must stop working.*

2. Receive Jesus and Yield to Him

The positive side is simple: *You receive Jesus and yield yourself without reservation to Him*. All God's grace is in Jesus Christ; He is the only channel of God's grace. When we receive Him, all the grace of God is made available to us. The first chapter of John's gospel makes this clear. Let's look at John 1:11–17.

We begin with verses 11–12: "He [Jesus] came to His own, and His own did not receive Him. But as many as received Him, to them He gave the right to become children of God, to those who believe in His name." The critical transaction is whether or not we receive Him. Once we receive Him, we are *given* the right to become children of God. It is a gift. We cannot earn it. The only thing we can do with a gift is to receive it.

Verse 13 indicates the result of receiving Him: "[These] were born, not of blood, nor of the will of the flesh, nor of the will of man, but of God." Those who receive Him are born anew. They experience a new inner spiritual transformation, renewal and rebirth. We need to see that this inner transformation is directly linked with the grace of God manifested in Jesus. Jesus is always the source of all grace.

John covers this in verse 14: "And the Word [this is the eternal Word, Jesus] became flesh and dwelt among us, and we beheld His glory, the glory as of the only begotten of the Father, full of grace and truth." Notice the emphasis on the glory of God that was upon Jesus: He was full of grace and truth.

176

Then John adds in verse 16: "And of His fullness we have all received, and grace for grace." In other words, when we receive Jesus, all God's fullness that is in Him is made available to us. For every grace there is in Jesus, a corresponding grace is made available to us.

Then John sums it up in the verse we have considered so many times, verse 17: "For the law was given through Moses, but grace and truth came through Jesus Christ."

The emphasis that John is making is on grace. "Full of grace and truth." "Grace upon grace." "Grace and truth." The point is clear: To receive that grace, we must receive Jesus. The decisive, positive aspect of this transaction, then, is *receiving Jesus* and *yielding to Him.*

It is not an issue of being holy, saying prayers, going to church or trying to become a better person. These are actions that may have some merit in their own place, but they are of no value in receiving grace. The key decisive transaction is yielding ourselves to Jesus, handing ourselves over to Him without reservation, and opening ourselves up to Him and all that He is able to bring into our lives.

Grace for Grace

The results of this transaction are twofold. First, there is a new birth; a completely new kind of life starts within us. It is not physical life; it is a spiritual life that will ultimately affect even our physical lives. Then, out of Jesus dwelling in us through the new birth, we receive of His fullness grace for grace. For every grace that is in Christ, the new birth opens the way for the corresponding grace to be manifested in us. It is all contained in Jesus.

Jesus is like a beautiful diamond with innumerable facets, all of which glitter and sparkle with beauty and with grace. Every facet of that diamond is a particular grace. Figuratively speaking, when we take that diamond in through the new birth, the way is open for that grace in all its facets to shine out of our lives.

I have proved this in my own experience time and time again. For many years my greatest personal problem was anger. I learned to yield to Jesus, however, and my problem of anger began to be replaced by His grace of gentleness. I can testify that this has worked in my life over the years. People who have known me only in the last years of my life would never believe that I had this problem with anger, because it has been replaced by the grace of God. I take no credit for this transformation; it has been by His grace. I did not earn it. I did not work for it. I just believed in His grace.

What if your problem is timidity? You yield to Jesus and the grace of His courage is made available to you. As you believe, your weakness of timidity is replaced by His grace of courage. The same would hold true if you have a problem with lust. Let the grace of the purity of Jesus be manifested in you.

In applying this, it is important that we never focus on the negative. Do not spend your time worrying about your problem, because that does not produce anything but more of the same problem. You turn away from the problem and yield to the corresponding grace of Jesus. If you have a problem with foolishness, accept the grace of wisdom that is in Jesus and begin to allow it to operate through you. You will be amazed at the results.

Worry is a common problem. First, stop worrying about worrying! It only compounds your worry. Yield to Jesus and let the grace of His peace take the place of the problem of your worrying. Usually we must yield to His grace again and again until it takes root and begins to rule in our lives. We must never become discouraged, however. We must do continually as John said, "Believe in Him." This is learning to rely on His grace day after day.

Learning to Rely on God's Grace

For most of us, learning to rely on God's grace is not an easy lesson! Our temptation is often to begin in God's grace, become a bit pleased with our progress, and think we are mature enough to handle things on our own. Without realizing it, we have ceased to rely on God's grace. Then, we are in trouble because we have begun to rely on our own carnal nature with all its inadequacies and failures. I want to suggest three simple, successive steps that can help us keep relying on God's grace.

Step One: Affirm Christ Living in You

Paul gives us a beautiful pattern of this affirmation:

I have been crucified with Christ; it is no longer I who live, but Christ lives in me; and the life which I now live in the flesh I live by faith in the Son of God, who loved me and gave Himself for me.

Galatians 2:20

As I affirm that I have been crucified with Christ, then I am no longer alive; now Christ is living in me. Now I will no longer meet life's problems as my old self; I meet life's problems as a person in whom Christ is living. He has become my life. We need to affirm this truth continually.

Every time you are under pressure and you think you cannot meet the challenges before you, speak as Paul spoke, "It's not I who live, but Christ who is living in me." It is important that we say these words out loud with our own mouths, actually verbalizing our faith. Verbalizing our faith is what the Bible calls "confession." The Greek word for *confession* literally means "to say the same thing as." Confession is saying the same thing with our mouths that the Bible declares and we believe in our heart. It is not sufficient merely to believe truth in our hearts. We must declare it with our mouths.

Step Two: Put No Confidence in the Flesh

We again look at the words of Paul, this time from Philippians 3:3: "For we are the circumcision, who worship God in the Spirit, rejoice in Christ Jesus, and have no confidence in the flesh."

There was a tremendous issue in Paul's day as to whether or not Gentile believers should be circumcised according to the Jewish tradition. The people who called themselves "the circumcision" regarded themselves as the people of God because they had been circumcised in their flesh.

Paul, however, states that true circumcision is not a physical act, but a spiritual one. He declares here that there are three marks of the truly circumcised people of God. *First*, they worship in the Spirit of God. They are not bound to an earthly place of worship because true worship is "in spirit and in truth" as Jesus declared to the Samaritan woman in Sychar (John 4:24). *Second*, those of the true circumcision rejoice, or boast, in Christ Jesus. They do not boast of their own righteousness, parentage, denomination or good works. They boast in Christ Jesus and His grace toward them. *Third*, they put no confidence in the flesh. They *deliberately declare* that they do not rely on their own ability, their own strength or their own righteousness.

Paul goes on in this passage to say, "If anybody could have relied on the flesh, it was I. I was of the people of Israel, a descendant of Abraham, tribe of Benjamin, circumcised the eighth day. In regard to the righteousness of the Law, I was faultless." But he then declared: "I have renounced confidence in all of that because it can't do for me what the grace of God can do."

In a certain sense, God is jealous of His grace. If you want His grace you must rely entirely and completely on His grace and nothing else. *You cannot mix grace and works.* This is why it is important that you declare, "I don't rely on my own good works, I don't rely on my own ability, I don't rely on my denomination. I rely on the grace of God in me."

Step Three: Rely on Christ's All-sufficiency

Again we quote from Paul a little further on in this letter: "I can do all things through Christ who strengthens me" (Philippians 4:13).

Paul declares, "I can do everything." This bold declaration is neither conceited nor proud because of the words that follow: *Through Christ who strengthens me.* Paul has already affirmed that it is not he who lives, it is Christ who lives in him. Based on this declaration he now says that with Christ living in him, he can face every situation and every problem. Wherever God places him, he knows he can handle the situation because it is Christ in him who gives him the strength.

It is important that you do not continually talk about your failures and your inabilities, because you have renounced them. Be positive according to the Word of God in what you speak about yourself. Declare continually with Paul, "I can do everything through Christ in me who gives me the strength."

I must emphasize that learning to rely on God's grace is a process that continues throughout our lives. In this process it is easy to become discouraged. One of the devil's strongest weapons against us is discouragement. When we get discouraged, then the enemy can do almost anything he wants with us. I have discovered two ways to guard against discouragement. If you should be discouraged at any time, or be tempted to be discouraged, let me offer you these two words of encouragement.

First, *when we are weak we are strong.* Paul discovered this:

And He said to me, "My grace is sufficient for you, for My strength is made perfect in weakness." Therefore most gladly I will rather boast in my infirmities, that the power of Christ may rest upon me. Therefore I take pleasure in infirmities, in reproaches, in needs, in persecutions, in distresses, for Christ's sake. For when I am weak, then I am strong.

2 Corinthians 12:9–10

Paul had discovered that when he felt weak he should not be discouraged, because when he was weak, he was strong. In a certain sense, it is good to feel weak. Because when you feel weak you are forced to rely on the grace of God.

In truth, God's grace is more easily manifested in those areas of our lives where we see our weakness than it is in those areas where we think we can handle the situation by ourselves. There will come times when we feel very weak and incapable. These are not the times to worry or give up. Rather, this is the time to rely all the more on the grace of God because God's grace is *offered to the weak*. Declare as Paul did, "I'm weak, that's true. But when I am weak, then I am strong."

Second, if you fail, do not become discouraged, because *your faith is still credited as righteousness even when you fail*. We see this truth in Romans 4:5: "But to him who does not work but believes on Him who justifies the ungodly, his faith is accounted for righteousness."

Even when you are not doing the right thing, even when you are failing, if you continue believing and trusting God, your faith is still credited to you as righteousness. It is not *your* righteousness; it is given to you as a credit from God.

183

Here is a parable from contemporary culture that explains how this works. Today we use credit cards to make most of our purchases. We do not have the cash on hand, but we offer the credit card and it is accepted just as if it were cash. God has made His righteousness "credit card" available to us through our faith. Thus, when you fail in any situation, you have the privilege of just stretching out the Father's credit card and saying to the devil, "My faith is still credited to me as righteousness. God accepts responsibility for me even the way I am." When we do this we are relying continually on the grace of God.

Making Room for God's Grace

Once we begin to learn to rely on God's grace, we need to take it one step further and begin to *make room for God's grace*. Making room for God's grace requires overcoming one great barrier—our self-life. As long as we seek to maintain our old self-life there really is no room for God's grace to be seen in us.

In this respect the human life could be compared to film in a camera. The film is only designed for a single exposure. Once the film has been exposed to an image, it is impossible to impose another image over it and have a clear picture. To create a new image, you need a new piece of film. In like manner, once self has been exposed in an area of our lives, it is futile to try to bring forth the image of Jesus in its place. The new birth creates a new, clean section of "film" upon which there is room for a true, accurate representation of

Jesus. It is futile to try to superimpose Jesus on the film that still has the old self-image on it because all it produces is a blurred image in which nothing is clear.

This truth was implied in the passage we considered in the previous section where Paul says, "I have been crucified with Christ; it is no longer I who live, but Christ lives in me" (Galatians 2:20). I must accept my own death before the life of Jesus becomes effective in me. Paul illustrates the same principle in this passage:

> For we do not preach ourselves, but Christ Jesus the Lord, and ourselves your bondservants for Jesus' sake. For it is the God who commanded light to shine out of darkness, who has shone in our hearts to give the light of the knowledge of the glory of God in the face of Jesus Christ.
>
> 2 Corinthians 4:5–6

This is a remarkable statement when we consider who said it and the situation in which it was made. Paul, the proud former Pharisee, a self-righteous Jew, is writing to the Corinthian Christians and he says, "We are your bondservants [Greek: *slaves*] for Jesus' sake." We need to remember what kind of people the Corinthian Christians had been before we can fully evaluate what is involved in Paul's statement. Earlier Paul had reminded them of who they had been:

> Do you not know that the unrighteous will not inherit the kingdom of God? Do not be deceived. Neither fornicators, nor idolaters, nor adulterers, nor homosexuals, nor sodomites, nor thieves, nor covetous, nor drunkards, nor revilers, nor

extortioners will inherit the kingdom of God. And such were some of you.

1 Corinthians 6:9–11

The Corinthian Christians had been sexually immoral, idolaters, adulterers, male prostitutes, homosexuals, thieves, greedy, drunkards, slanderers and swindlers. To this group of people Paul, the proud, self-righteous Pharisee writes, "We are your bondservants, your slaves, for Jesus' sake." This is one of the clearest statements of the grace of God in all of Scripture. Apart from the grace of God there is no way that a man like Paul could ever have been changed to this extent. His own religious practices would never have achieved it. Formerly, he would have pulled the hem of his robe away from them if he passed them on the street. Yet here he is saying to these same people, "We're your slaves; we're here to serve you; we want to do you good."

Paul lists three steps that brought him to this place of grace. The first is *the denial of self*: "We don't preach ourselves." The second is *acknowledging the Lordship of Jesus*: "Christ Jesus as Lord." And the third is *considering "ourselves as your slaves."*

Paul goes on to emphasize that this miraculous grace of God is contained in earthen vessels so that we always remain continually dependent on grace.

But we have this treasure in earthen vessels, that the excellence of the power may be of God and not of us. We are hard-pressed on every side, yet not crushed; we are perplexed, but not in despair; persecuted, but not forsaken; struck down, but not destroyed—always carrying about in the body the dying of the Lord Jesus, that the life of Jesus also may be manifested in our body. For we who live are always delivered to death for Jesus' sake, that the life of Jesus also may be manifested in our mortal flesh. So then death is working in us, but life in you.

2 Corinthians 4:7–12

The last short sentence is significant. "Death works in us, but life in you." We cannot become channels for the life and the grace of Christ until death has worked in us, until we deny ourselves, until we have seen our old self as crucified on the cross with Christ. Then we can say as Paul, "I am crucified with Christ. I've come to the end of my own life. I've shared that shameful death with Jesus on the cross. Now it is not I who live."

Once we have come to the end of our own sufficiency, our own righteousness and our own strength, then the life of God flows through us to others. We become channels of divine supernatural life and grace. Through my own experience in many years of ministry, I have learned that I am usually the most successful when I am the most inconvenienced, the most overtaxed, or when I would most gladly be doing something else. It is through the denial of myself in practical ways, which results in the death of self, that the life of Jesus can be manifested.

We must remember that we are just earthen vessels. Pressures, problems and trials are bound to come. They are merely a way of reminding us that it is not we who are living, but Jesus who is living in us. God's strength is made perfect in our weakness. The pressures we face are designed to keep us relying more and more on the grace of God, thus making more and more room for His grace to flow in and through us.

Boasting of Grace Alone

This chapter has led us through a progression of growing in grace, from humbling ourselves to receive the grace of God to making room for His grace to work in and through us by denying ourselves. This final step is, in many ways, a culmination of every step. It is *boasting only in the grace of God.*

The grace of God leaves no room for boasting—except about the grace of God! In reality, if we are truly living in the grace of God, grace is the only theme about which we can boast. We have nothing left of our own goodness, our own righteousness or our own wisdom to boast about. Paul repeats this theme in several passages of the New Testament: "Where is boasting then? It is excluded. By what law? Of works? No, but by the law of faith. Therefore we conclude that a man is justified by faith apart from the deeds of the law" (Romans 3:27–28).

Paul makes it clear that if we have been justified by faith without keeping the Law then we have nothing about which we can boast. Boasting is excluded by the principle of faith.

In Romans 4, Paul goes on to apply this specifically to Abraham. It was important for Paul to prove that Abraham was accepted by God based on the principle of faith alone, because Abraham was the father of the race of Israel. By pointing to Abraham's experience, Paul is presenting a key by which Israel could understand her own experience. Paul is careful to point out, therefore, that Abraham had nothing to boast about. He, too, was justified by faith without works, as we saw in an earlier chapter.

> What then shall we say that Abraham our father has found according to the flesh? For if Abraham was justified by works, he has something to boast about, but not before God. For what does the Scripture say? "Abraham believed God, and it was accounted to him for righteousness."
>
> Romans 4:1–3

Abraham received righteousness from God, not on the basis of keeping any law or performing good works, but simply because he believed in God's grace. And on the basis of his faith, he was credited with righteousness. Abraham received that wonderful "credit card" of God's righteousness. As I mentioned before, even when we are not measuring up to how we ought to live, our faith is still credited for righteousness. We can never pay in the "cash" of good works; but we can extend God's "credit card" of righteousness.

In his letter to the Corinthian church, Paul reminds the Corinthian Christians what type of people they had been before they came to Christ. Then he points out the same lesson: There is not any room left for boasting.

> Brothers, think of what you were when you were called. Not many of you were wise by human standards; not many were influential; not many were of noble birth. But God chose the foolish things of the world to shame the wise;

God chose the weak things of the world to shame the strong. He chose the lowly things of this world and the despised things—and the things that are not—to nullify the things that are, so that no one may boast before him. It is because of him that you are in Christ Jesus, who has become for us wisdom from God—that is, our righteousness, holiness and redemption. Therefore, as it is written: "Let him who boasts boast in the Lord."

1 Corinthians 1:26–31, NIV

Paul begins by listing the three main qualities that cause men to trust in themselves: wisdom or education, influence (social or political) and noble birth. Paul reminds the Corinthian believers that most of them could not boast on any of those three scores. But Paul goes on to say that God has chosen the foolish things, the weak things, the lowly things, the despised things and even things that are not, just to bring to nothing all the things that are considered worthwhile by the world.

Then Paul gives the reason why God has done this. It is because we have nothing of ourselves—it is not our own righteousness, our own holiness or our own redemption. In the wisdom of God, Jesus Christ has been made to us all these things: righteousness, holiness and redemption. It is God's grace in us that produces these things.

Then Paul draws this conclusion: "Therefore, as it is written: 'Let him who boasts boast in the Lord.'" We have nothing in this life about which we may boast. As we understand fully the grace of God, we are left with only His grace about which we may boast in time or in eternity. Paul carries this a step further in Galatians 6:14 with what I consider to be a most amazing statement: "But God forbid that I should boast except in the cross of our Lord Jesus Christ, by whom the world has been crucified to me, and I to the world."

In the ancient world of Paul's day, the cross was the ultimate emblem of shame and degradation. Under Roman law a Roman citizen could not be crucified. They were executed in some other manner because crucifixion downgraded the dignity of Roman citizenship. Paul, you will remember, was not executed by crucifixion because he was a Roman citizen. In this statement, Paul says that he will boast only in the most shameful thing in the culture of his day—a cross. Paul boasts in the crucifixion of the Lord Jesus Christ, however, because it is through the cross that the grace of God is made available to him.

All the glory (which is another way of saying, "boasting") throughout eternity goes to God's grace.

> [God] having predestined us to adoption as sons by Jesus Christ to Himself, according to the good pleasure of His will, to the praise of the glory of His grace, by which He made us accepted in the Beloved.
>
> Ephesians 1:5–6

Everything God is doing to us is ultimately designed to bring praise, or boasting, to the glory of His grace, which He has freely bestowed upon us. All legitimate boasting ultimately relates somehow to the grace of God. Paul emphasizes this a little further on:

In [Christ] also we have obtained an inheritance, being predestined according to the purpose of Him who works all things according to the counsel of His will, that we who first trusted in Christ should be to the praise of His glory.

verses 11–12

In other words, all is destined to bring praise and glory to God. Paul continues with the same theme:

But God, who is rich in mercy, because of His great love with which He loved us, even when we were dead in trespasses, made us alive together with Christ (by grace you have been saved), and raised us up together, and made us sit together in the heavenly places in Christ Jesus, that in the ages to come He might show the exceeding riches of His grace in His kindness toward us in Christ Jesus.

Ephesians 2:4–7

God selects the lowest, the least worthy and the weakest. Then He bestows His grace upon them, transforms them, raises them up with Christ and seats them with Christ on His throne in heavenly places. Please notice that His ultimate purpose is that through all ages He will demonstrate the surpassing riches of His grace in His kindness toward us. His grace will be the ultimate theme of the ages to come.

The true extent of God's grace is difficult to comprehend. He takes the lowest and lifts them to the highest; always with the purpose that all the glory should go to His grace and none of it to us. When we understand the extent and magnitude of God's grace—when we realize that we have become, through no effort or merit of our own, the unworthy recipients of the full measure of His grace—is it any wonder that His grace must be our one and only boast?

11

The Presence of Grace

In this final chapter, I want to consider a few of the results of having the grace of God operating in our lives. The first, and in some ways the most meaningful result, is that God's grace brings His very presence into our lives.

Grace Is a "Presence"

In chapter 4 we considered the blessing of the Levitical priests: "The LORD bless you and keep you; the LORD make His face shine upon you, and be gracious to you; the LORD lift up His countenance upon you, and give you peace" (Numbers 6:24–26).

In the middle of this passage we find the phrase *the Lord be gracious to you*. We could paraphrase this as, "the Lord extend, or exercise, His grace toward you—His free unmerited favor." It is important, as we noted before, to keep in mind that the extension of His grace is directly connected with the Lord's face. "The Lord make His face shine upon you, and be gracious to you; the Lord lift up His countenance upon you." In other words, the Lord's favor is connected with the way He looks at us. Sovereignly, He looks upon us with favor. As He begins to look upon us with favor, we are singled out, our destiny has changed and we become different from the people around us.

A good example, as we pointed out, was Noah. Genesis 6:8 says that "Noah found grace [or favor] in the eyes of the Lord." The favor Noah found in God's eyes distinguished him from all the other men of his generation. As a result of the Lord looking upon Noah in grace, Noah's destiny was changed.

In the Levitical blessing, after those words, "the Lord lift up His countenance upon you," we have the culmination: "and give you peace [shalom]." Shalom also means "welfare," "health" and "prosperity." Shalom peace is always the outcome of grace. Indeed, apart from God's grace we can never really know true peace.

It is important to see that grace is more than a mere attitude of God. When God looks upon us with His favor, He transmits something of Himself to us. In His grace we are surrounded with a different atmosphere in which we are protected. Grace is not just a legal transaction; it is a very real impartation of God's very presence. God's eyes look upon us and transmit His love, His mercy and, above all, His presence. The grace of God brings the presence of God into our lives in a way that changes the atmosphere around us.

I like to picture the operation of His presence something like this. Envision a hot, humid day in which everybody is driving around in cars that are not air-conditioned. We, however, have an air-conditioned car. So while everybody else is miserable, hot and perspiring, we are cool and restful because we have a different atmosphere. In a similar manner, God's grace surrounds us with a different atmosphere, protecting us from what others experience as part of living in a fallen world.

Seeing grace in this way explains many of the expressions used by the writers of the New Testament, which, apart from understanding grace as a palpable presence, we could not fully appreciate. We have already noted that *grace and peace* was both the normal greeting that opened a New Testament epistle and the benediction that closed it. Paul begins his letter to the Romans, for example, with the salutation, "Grace to you and peace from God our Father and the Lord Jesus Christ" (Romans 1:7). Grace comes to us from God the Father, through the Lord Jesus Christ the Son. Grace is His favor and it brings His peace, His wholeness, His completeness and His all-sufficiency.

Paul then closes his letter to Rome in a similar fashion, where he makes a bold statement of faith and brings two ideas together that are significant: "And the God of peace will crush Satan under your feet shortly. The grace of our Lord Jesus Christ be with you. Amen" (Romans 16:20). In other words, Paul says it is God's grace, favor and presence that will make his readers victorious over Satan. This pattern is repeated by Paul in his second letter to Timothy: "To Timothy, a beloved son: Grace, mercy, and peace from God the Father and Christ Jesus our Lord" (2 Timothy 1:2).

In this greeting, Paul adds one more blessing to grace and peace—he adds mercy. But we see again that grace always comes first and all other blessings flow out of grace. At the end of his letter to Timothy, Paul says in closing: "The Lord Jesus Christ be with your spirit. Grace be with you. Amen" (2 Timothy 4:22). Paul gives this blessing in a manner that suggests that the presence of the Lord is His grace abiding with us. Paul speaks about grace as something that actually accompanies us and is present with us. "Grace *be with* you."

Paul speaks of the presence of grace in his own testimony about his labors for the Lord: "By the grace of God I am what I am, and His grace toward me was not in vain; but I labored more abundantly than they all, yet not I, but the grace of God which was with me" (1 Corinthians 15:10).

In Paul's testimony he uses the word *grace* three times in this one verse. "By the *grace* of God I am what I am . . . His *grace* toward me . . . the *grace* of God which was with me." As Paul explains his success in Christian ministry, he makes no claims for himself. He claims success for the grace of God. He states, "The grace of God was with me, like a presence, something that followed me and overshadowed me, keeping company with me wherever I went and labored for the Lord."

Two beautiful pictures from the Old Testament portray God's grace as a presence with us. The first from Psalm 5:12: "For You, O LORD, will bless the righteous; with favor You will surround him as with a shield."

As I have mentioned previously, the word *favor* is an alternative word for *grace*, and especially in the Old Testament, the two words are used almost interchangeably. As David expresses so clearly here, the grace (or favor) of God is not just a theological concept; it is a real presence that surrounds us. His grace protects us, it enfolds us, it drives back the evil forces that oppose us. As you read this, think of yourself as being surrounded with a shield that protects you from harm and danger—spiritual, emotional, physical and even financial. There is no evil force that can penetrate that shield of the grace of God if you will receive His grace by faith, depend upon it and believe it is with you.

A second beautiful picture of grace as the Lord's presence is in Proverbs 16:15, "In the light of the king's face is life, and his favor is like a cloud of the latter rain." Consider the fact that when we are referring to a king in this passage, we are talking about Jesus, who is not just any king. He is the King of all kings. "In the light of His face is life." When He lifts up His face upon us and looks upon us with favor, that is life.

The writer says that the favor of a king is like a cloud with the spring rain. In the land of Israel, rain is one of the greatest blessings; it is never unwanted. It is something that those who live in Israel cry out for. And the most blessed rain of all is the spring rain or the latter rain, the one that brings the greatest fruitfulness and the surest prospect of a good harvest. A cloud that brings the spring rain, therefore, is something that people long for. It is the assurance of blessing, of fruitfulness and of God's abundant provision for His people. God's favor is like that cloud that promises the coming of the spring rains.

As you consider the grace that comes to you through Jesus Christ, therefore, envision yourself surrounded by a cloud of His presence like a cloud of spring rain—the cloud of God's favor overshadowing you and protecting you.

Grace Teaches Godliness

A particular aspect of God's grace that surprises many people is that grace teaches us. Paul expresses this aspect of grace in his letter to Titus, who was a young man in the ministry serving as a pastor and personal representative of Paul. In the second chapter of his letter to Titus, Paul is telling Titus how to best care for God's people and how to bring out the best in each of them. In this context Paul addresses various different categories within the total congregation (the young men, the old men, the older women and so on) and in each case Paul tells Titus what he is to teach them. At the close of the chapter he goes on to say, "Remember it is God's grace that teaches all of us" (see Titus 2:11–12). In other words, Titus is to be an instrument of the grace of God in teaching what Paul tells him to teach.

But as for you, speak [or teach] the things which are proper for sound doctrine: that the older men be sober, reverent, temperate, sound in faith, in love, in patience.

Titus 2:1–2

The older women likewise, that they be reverent in behavior, not slanderers, not given to much wine, teachers of good things.

verse 3

Likewise, exhort [exhortation is a form of teaching] the young men to be sober-minded, in all things showing yourself to be a pattern of good works.

verses 6–7

Exhort bondservants to be obedient to their own masters, to be well pleasing in all things, not answering back.

verse 9

For each separate group, there is a particularly appropriate emphasis on the teaching that they need. Paul then goes on to close the chapter with a beautiful picture of the grace of God. What he is really saying is that all these different aspects of teaching proceed from one source—the *grace of God*.

For the grace of God that brings salvation has appeared to all men, teaching us that, denying ungodliness and worldly lusts, we should live soberly, righteously, and godly in the present age, looking for the blessed hope and glorious appearing of our great God and Savior Jesus Christ, who gave Himself for us, that He might redeem us from every lawless deed and purify for Himself His own special people, zealous for good works.

verses 11–14

Consider some of the lessons grace teaches us. As you do, ask yourself if you are allowing the grace of God to teach you these truths.

First on Paul's list is a powerful principle. Grace teaches us to say no to ungodliness and worldly passion. We will never get far in life if we do not know how to say no and mean it. There are going to be situations in which we are confronted with enticements of evil, or with an easy option in a difficult situation that may not be God's solution. We are never going to succeed in life if we have not learned to reject evil in such a way that the devil and everybody else knows we really mean it. Grace teaches us to say no to ungodliness and worldly passion.

Second on Paul's list, grace teaches us to live self-controlled, upright, godly lives. Some people seem to believe that grace means you can do anything you like or anything that feels good. Such beliefs are the exact opposite of what God states in His Word. If you are being taught by grace, it will teach you to live in a self-controlled, upright and godly manner.

Third on the list, grace teaches us to wait for the appearing of Jesus Christ. It gives us an objective to which our lives are directed—the blessed hope of the appearing of the great God and our Savior, Jesus Christ. I believe a person who is not excited and focused upon the return of Jesus is not really living in the grace of God.

202

Fourth on Paul's list, grace reminds us that Jesus died to redeem us and purify us from all wickedness. The whole emphasis in this passage is turning from wickedness, being redeemed from it and being purified.

Fifth and last on his list, grace teaches us that we ought to be eager to do what is good. This is a different picture of grace from what some people hear in their churches. Grace never sets a lower standard than the Law; grace sets a higher standard. As we have seen, however, the difference is that the Law teaches from *without* while grace teaches from *within*. Law is commandments, which are held up before you and say, "Do this! Don't do that!" You may say, "Fine, that's good," but there is something in you that cannot respond, because there is a rebel in there who just will not yield to the Law.

Grace, however, comes into us and changes the rebel from within. Grace begins to speak to that converted rebel: "This is the way you need to respond. This is the way through this difficulty." Then, when you are confronted with a temptation, grace enables you to say, "No!" This is how grace teaches us. If we do not allow grace to teach us, we end up abusing the very grace that was intended to make us free.

Today, just as it was in Paul's day, there is the temptation to use the grace of God to give license to the old rebel to live any way he wants. There are two warnings in the New Testament against abusing God's grace. In 2 Corinthians 6:1, Paul says: "We then, as workers together with Him also plead with you not to receive the grace of God in vain."

It is possible to receive the grace of God in vain. What does that mean? I believe it means you lay claim to God's grace,

His grace begins to operate in your life, but you refuse to let grace teach you how you should live. By refusing to come under the discipline of grace, you go on living your own way, pleasing yourself and claiming to be in the grace of God. But you are deceiving yourself. If you are living in the grace of God, the truths that grace teaches you will be manifested in your life. If they are not manifested in your life, you are receiving the grace of God in vain.

Likewise, Jude 4 contains a very strong warning against abusing the grace of God:

> For certain men have crept in unnoticed, who long ago were marked out for this condemnation, ungodly men, who turn the grace of our God into lewdness and deny the only Lord God and our Lord Jesus Christ.

Tragically, the abuse of grace Jude is warning about in this passage continues to occur in churches and other Christian ministries today. Many who claim to be committed believers also claim to be in the grace of God, but they are living loose, immoral lives. Scripture says they have changed the grace of God into a license for immorality.

I believe the only way to avoid abusing the grace of God is to allow that very grace to teach us. We are submitting ourselves to grace by allowing His instruction from the Scriptures to show us the kind of life we ought to lead. Then we allow grace to supply us with the ability to lead that kind of life. Grace is the perfect teacher, because it not only instructs us, but then gives us the ability to live in accordance with that instruction.

Grace Produces Thankfulness

In the previous chapter, I pointed out what happens when we receive Jesus Christ. All of God's fullness, which is in Christ, is made available to us. John wrote, "And of His fullness we have all received, and grace for grace" (John 1:16). In other words, for every grace that is in Jesus, there is a corresponding grace that begins to operate in our lives. One vital area of our lives that is affected when grace begins to operate in us is our lips—our speech begins to change.

There is a beautiful prophetic picture of Jesus Christ given to us in the Psalms. The psalmist is looking forward in the Spirit of God to the coming of the Messiah, and he sings a beautiful song of praise to Him: "You are fairer than the sons of men; grace is poured upon Your lips; therefore God has blessed You forever" (Psalm 45:2).

By revelation, the psalmist sees the grace of God upon this beautiful person, the Messiah. Notice that the first area that attracts him is the lips of the Messiah. "Grace is poured upon Your lips." The gospel of John records an incident toward the end of Jesus' life when the religious leaders sent a group of officers to arrest Jesus. When the officers returned without Jesus, the leaders asked them, "Why didn't you bring Him?" Their reply was, "No man ever spoke like this Man!" (John 7:46). They recognized that there was grace poured upon His lips.

Then the psalmist goes on to say: "Therefore God has blessed You forever." It is important to notice the *therefore*. Jesus was not blessed because He was a favorite Son; He was blessed because He met the conditions to be blessed. The first condition, which the psalmist notes, was the beauty upon His lips, or the grace of His speech. Because of that grace upon His lips, God blessed Him forever. With the corresponding grace upon our lips, we qualify for the same blessing. Jesus was not blessed because of favoritism; He was blessed because He qualified for it. When we qualify by allowing grace to be upon our lips, we receive the same blessing.

This brings us to a fundamental connection between two phrases that are common in the Scriptures: *to have grace* and *to be thankful*. This connection is uniquely illustrated by the manner in which different translators of the New Testament have translated a single verse: Hebrews 12:28. The New King James reads:

> Therefore, since we are receiving a kingdom which cannot be shaken, let us have grace, by which we may serve God acceptably with reverence and godly fear.

Notice the phrase *"let us have grace, by which we may serve God."* Again, it is obvious that grace produces godliness; there is no other way to interpret this phrase. Here is that same verse in the New American Standard version:

> Therefore, since we receive a kingdom which cannot be shaken, let us show gratitude, by which we may offer to God an acceptable service with reverence and awe.

Do you see the difference? The New King James says, "let us have grace" and the New American Standard says, "let us show gratitude." You may wonder why the translators could not agree. The truth is, they *did* agree. They simply chose different aspects of the same word. In the Greek language in Paul's time, *to have grace* also meant to say *thank you. To have grace* was the standard phrase for being thankful. The point is this: You cannot have grace without being thankful. An unthankful person has run out of the grace of God.

I have studied a number of languages beginning with Latin and Greek as a youth, and several modern languages as I grew older. There is a group of languages called the "Romance languages," which are rooted in Latin. In every one of them, the word for *thank you* is directly related to the word for *grace*. In French, "Thanks be to God" is *grâce á Dieu*. When the Italians want to say, "Thank you," they say, "*Grazie*." In Spanish, you say, "*Gracias*." In each, the word is rooted in the word *grace*. You cannot have grace without gratitude; the words are tied together. One of the first manifestations of grace, therefore, is being grateful. And the primary way in which we give thanks is with our speech. When we are no longer truly thankful in our speech, we have moved out of grace.

Paul further addresses the issue of how the grace of God affects our speech:

> But above all these things put on love, which is the bond of perfection. And let the peace of God rule in your hearts, to which also you were called in one body; and be thankful. Let the word of Christ dwell in you richly in all wisdom, teaching and admonishing one another in psalms and hymns and spiritual songs, singing with grace in your hearts to the Lord.
>
> Colossians 3:14–16

207

While the New King James translation says *singing with grace in your hearts*, the New American Standard reads *singing with thankfulness in your hearts*. Please notice the different translations of the same word. If you are in the grace of God, you will be thankful. Thankfulness of speech is a necessary result of the grace of God. It cannot be otherwise.

We have seen that the grace of God teaches us, and Paul here takes this concept a step further. He points out that when we are in the grace of God, we can teach others. He says, "Let the word of Christ richly dwell within you, with all wisdom, teaching and admonishing one another with psalms and hymns and spiritual songs." A person in the grace of God will be thankful. He will be full of praise, he will want to sing, he will give vocal expression to what is in his heart, and he will have something to pass on to his fellow believers. He will be able to teach and admonish his fellow believers out of the grace of God that is operating in his heart, which is expressing itself primarily through thankfulness.

Paul states further that grace in our speech is like the salt in our food: "Let your speech always be with grace, seasoned with salt, that you may know how you ought to answer each one" (Colossians 4:6). The function of salt when added to our food is to make it flavorful and attractive. Salt brings out the various flavors in food that we enjoy savoring to the full. Grace has the same function in relationship to our speech. Grace is like salt sprinkled on our lips. It makes our words attractive and creates an appetite in those who hear to want more of the grace of God.

Grace Produces Generosity

One of the most beautiful manifestations of God's grace is generosity. Again we turn to Jesus as the pattern, because when Jesus comes into our lives the grace of God comes with Him: grace for grace. For every grace in Jesus, there is a corresponding grace that is manifested in us through Jesus being in us. And the grace of generosity finds its perfect expression in Jesus.

There is an example of this expressed by Paul in his second letter to the Corinthians. He is writing about an offering for the poor believers in Jerusalem that was being taken up among the churches in the Gentile world. Paul is writing to these believers in Corinth and explaining the principle of this offering as well as the more general principles of godly giving. "For you know the grace of our Lord Jesus Christ, that though He was rich, yet for your sakes He became poor, that you through His poverty might become rich" (2 Corinthians 8:9). Because of the grace that was in Jesus, He laid aside His infinite wealth and became poor on our behalf. His motive was that through His poverty, we might become rich.

Grace makes us givers. People who do not enjoy giving have very little of the grace of God working in their lives. Earlier in this chapter Paul had written about how the attitude of joyful giving will be produced by the grace of God.

Moreover, brethren, we make known to you the grace of God bestowed on the churches of Macedonia: that in a great trial of affliction the abundance of their joy and their deep poverty abounded in the riches of their liberality. For I bear witness

209

that according to their ability, yes, and beyond their ability,
they were freely willing.

2 Corinthians 8:1–3

First, we need to see that the generosity of the Macedonian believers was an expression of grace. Paul writes
about the "grace of God bestowed on the churches," which
was expressed in the way they gave. Next, it is important
to note that the churches did not give out of abundance or
from surplus. Paul notes that they were under severe trial
themselves, and their condition was one of extreme poverty.
Yet, out of their poverty the grace of God welled up through
them in rich generosity. Grace is never limited to what we
think we can do. When we have worked out what we think
we might be able to give, we have yet to touch the grace of
God, because the grace of God goes beyond what we think
we can do.

Paul writes this about the churches in Macedonia: "I testify
that they gave as much as they were able." That was their
own ability. Then he adds, ". . . and even beyond their ability." That was where grace began. Grace always begins when
we have reached the limit of our own ability.

Paul then applies this example of the Macedonian churches
as a principle to the church of Corinth.

So we urged Titus, that as he had begun, so he would also
complete this grace in you as well. But as you abound in everything—in faith, in speech, in knowledge, in all diligence, and
in your love for us—see that you abound in this grace also.

2 Corinthians 8:6–7

210

Paul challenges the church in Corinth that as the grace of God was already manifested in many areas—in faith, in speech, in knowledge, in diligence and in love—that they should also be complete in this aspect of the grace of God. "See that you abound also in this grace of giving."

Paul goes on in the next chapter to show us that the grace of God will provide both the motivation and the means for giving.

> And God is able to make all grace abound toward you, that you, always having all sufficiency in all things, may have an abundance for every good work. As it is written: "He has dispersed abroad, He has given to the poor; His righteousness endures forever."
>
> 2 Corinthians 9:8–9

Paul states that grace makes total provision for all our needs. Through grace, therefore, we do not merely have enough for ourselves; there is an overflow to give for every good work. To reinforce this principle, Paul quotes from Psalm 112:9, stating that our righteousness is established and made permanent as we give. The individual pictured in Psalm 112 had scattered his gifts abroad to the poor; he had given lavishly and generously in grace; and as a result, the assurance was "his righteousness endures forever." The grace of giving establishes our righteousness.

Jesus Himself establishes a similar principle in relationship to grace as He sends out the apostles for the first time with the message of the Gospel. Here is His instruction: "And as you go, preach, saying, 'The kingdom of heaven is at hand.'

Heal the sick, cleanse the lepers, raise the dead, cast out demons. Freely you have received, freely give"(Matthew 10:7–8).

Jesus is speaking to His disciples about the abilities He has given to them to minister the Gospel by driving out demons and healing the sick. He says to them: "It didn't cost you anything. You didn't have to pay for it. You received it out of the grace of God as a free gift. Minister it in the same way you have received it. Freely you have received, freely give." This applies in every area of our lives. Whatever we receive freely from God, we ought to give away as freely as we have received. We cannot minister God's grace in a different way from the manner in which we received it.

Jesus also says,

"Give, and it will be given to you: good measure, pressed down, shaken together, and running over will be put into your bosom. For with the same measure that you use, it will be measured back to you."

Luke 6:38

Again, giving is the key to receiving. The measure with which we give is the measure by which it will be given back to us. And, as a result of gracious giving, we will get back more than we gave in proportion to the way that we gave.

By way of illustration, there are two seas in the Holy Land—the Sea of Galilee and the Dead Sea. They are both fed from the River Jordan, but there is a great difference between them. The Sea of Galilee is fresh and beautiful; it is full of life. The Dead Sea, as its name implies, is totally dead. What is the difference? They both receive from the same river, but the Sea of Galilee gives out, allowing the River Jordan to flow out as well as in. On the other hand, the Dead Sea gives nothing out. The River Jordan only flows into the Dead Sea, not out. The key to life is receiving *and* giving. The way to death is receiving but not giving.

This principle is summed up in this Scripture:

> There is one who scatters, yet increases more; and there is one who withholds more than is right, but it leads to poverty. The generous soul will be made rich, and he who waters will also be watered himself.
>
> Proverbs 11:24–25

Make a decision to be generous. Do not hold on and say, "I may not get any more." The measure with which you give will be the measure with which you receive.

Grace Is Sufficient

The theme of grace can be summed up by one simple but all-embracing statement: *God's grace is sufficient.* This truth is illustrated in the testimony of the apostle Paul as he writes about the sufficiency of grace from personal experience. Out of the tremendous pressures and needs of his life, he comes up with this triumphant truth: *God's grace is sufficient.*

In 2 Corinthians, Paul has been speaking about the tremendous revelations he received from God. But he balances this by saying that lest he should become proud, God let these revelations be accompanied by a particular force of evil that troubled him continually, one that Paul called a messenger of Satan.

> And lest I should be exalted above measure by the abundance of the revelations, a thorn in the flesh was given to me, a messenger of Satan to buffet me, lest I be exalted above measure. Concerning this thing I pleaded with the Lord three times that it might depart from me. And He said to me, "My grace is sufficient for you, for My strength is made perfect in weakness." Therefore most gladly I will rather boast in my infirmities, that the power of Christ may rest upon me. Therefore I take pleasure in infirmities, in reproaches, in needs, in persecutions, in distresses, for Christ's sake. For when I am weak, then I am strong.
>
> 2 Corinthians 12:7–10

When the grace of God is operating in our lives, we are not limited to our own resources. In fact, God's grace begins just where our own resources end. As long as we can handle the situation in our own ability, in our own strength and in our own wisdom, we do not need God's grace. When we come to the end of our own ability, strength and wisdom, however, that is where God's grace comes into operation.

Paul says in essence, "If you want the grace of God in an abundant measure, then get in a hard place in the will of God." The more difficult and impossible our circumstances become, the greater then will be the measure of God's grace available to us.

Take to heart what Paul says here. "I take pleasure in infirmities, in reproaches, in needs, in persecutions, in distresses." Surely, this does not make sense! How could Paul delight in things like that? Paul says, "I've learned a lesson. Difficulties make me weak; they bring me to the end of my own ability. However, when I am weak, then I am strong!"

God's grace will not force its way through our strength. As long as we are strong, God's grace stays in the background. But when we are weak while moving in the will of God, when we have run out of all our own ability, that is where God's grace comes flooding in. The greater the need, the greater the measure of God's grace.

There is an example of this principle from the ministry of Jesus. There were two occasions when Jesus fed large multitudes supernaturally. On the first occasion He fed five thousand men with five loaves and two fishes and the disciples took up twelve full baskets of leftovers after everybody had eaten all they wanted. On the second occasion, Jesus fed four thousand men with seven loaves and "a few" fishes and there were seven baskets left over. It is interesting to note that there were fewer baskets of leftovers following the second feeding. I believe this is significant. Please take note: The challenge was smaller the second time; there were fewer people (one thousand fewer men), and there were greater resources (seven loaves and a few fishes), but they had fewer baskets left over.

On the first occasion the situation was more impossible, yet, they took up more baskets of leftovers. The lesson is quite clear: The greater the impossibility, the greater the grace of God.

Never allow yourself to develop an attitude where you say, "Well, this situation is so hard, it's so impossible, there's nothing to be done about it." Cultivate the attitude of Paul:

"Praise God, the situation is a total impossibility. I'm delighted, because this makes real room for the grace of God to be manifested in this situation." We must grasp this fact and hold on to it: *The grace of God lifts us above our own natural ability.*

Stewards of His Grace

In 1 Peter 4:10, the apostle Peter writes: "As each one has received a gift, minister it to one another, as good stewards of the manifold grace of God." The Greek word for *gift* is *charisma*. It is formed directly from the Greek word for *grace, charis. Charisma*, a gift in this sense, is God's grace made specific in a particular form or manifestation. So Peter says each one of us has our own particular manifestation of God's grace.

In other words, as God's grace comes into our lives, it is manifested partly through gifts that God gives us as special abilities. And as we exercise these abilities, we are acting as stewards of God's manifold grace. The word *manifold* is a vivid word that means "many-sided." There is no limit to the different aspects of God's grace. Whatever aspect of God's grace is operating in us, we minister out of that to others.

There is a beautiful little definition of *grace*:

*G*od's
*R*iches
*A*t
*C*hrist's
*E*xpense

216

We need to lay hold of the fact that God is our source of riches. He is not poor. He is not in danger of going bankrupt, and He will never run out of grace. The source is inexhaustible.

In concluding this book on the grace of God, I want to lay fresh and final emphasis on the fact that God's grace is rich. I want to quote two passages from Ephesians in this context.

The first is: "In Him [Christ] we have redemption through His blood, the forgiveness of sins, according to the riches of His grace" (Ephesians 1:7). Notice that our forgiveness comes out of the riches of God's grace. His grace is not something He hands out meagerly; it is rich.

The second is: "[God] raised us up together . . . that in the ages to come He might show the exceeding riches of His grace in His kindness toward us in Christ Jesus" (Ephesians 2:7).

It is typical of Paul that the further he goes with something that is related to God, the more excited he gets about it and the larger his vision becomes. In Ephesians 1, he speaks of "the riches of God's grace." By the time he has gotten to the next chapter, he is so taken up with this theme that now he says, "the exceeding [or incomparable] riches of God's grace." There is nothing on earth with which to compare the riches of God's grace. We can think of the richest patron, the most generous philanthropist or the largest bank. But nothing offers any standard of comparison for the riches of God's grace.

In practical application this means the more we draw on God's grace the more there is left. It is not diminished, nor lessened to any degree—*the grace of God is inexhaustible.*

Let me present this thought to you: "The *will* of God will never place you where the *grace* of God cannot keep you." If you are in the will of God, no matter how strange, unfamiliar or difficult the situation may be, if you come to the end of all your own strength and resources, bear this in mind: "The *will* of God will never place you where the *grace* of God cannot keep you."

Receive His Grace

In closing this book I want to give you the opportunity to respond to the grace that has been offered to you in Christ. As I have ministered the Word of God through the years, I have endeavored to move beyond merely giving lectures about spiritual truth. I always seek to give those receiving the teaching the opportunity to respond and apply what has been taught in a personal and meaningful manner.

As you have read through these pages, you may have come to the realization that in some measure you have been trying to earn, or to become worthy of, the blessings of God in your life by keeping rules, or by endeavoring to measure up to some standard of what a "good Christian" should be. You may feel, at least in some areas of your life, like a "tree in the desert"—never fully experiencing the presence of God's grace and favor in the atmosphere surrounding your life.

If you can identify with this in any way, then I would encourage you to make a decision to *stop working* and to *receive by faith* the grace that God has freely bestowed on you in Christ Jesus. I would encourage you to pray the following prayer out loud:

Dear Father,

I come to You now in the name of Your Son, the Lord Jesus. I confess that I have tried to earn Your blessings and favor by my own efforts. I have tried to attain a personal standard of righteousness that I thought would make me acceptable to You. I ask forgiveness in the name of Jesus. Would You please deliver me from any form of darkness that has surrounded me because of the curse of the broken law?

I humble myself before You, and I confess that I am receiving Your grace and favor by faith. I make the decision to stop working for Your favor. And I humbly declare that I am righteous before You, not based on anything I have done, but on the righteousness of Christ, which has been given to me based on His finished work on the cross on my behalf. I confess that it is a free gift, not bestowed upon me because of any righteousness or merit on my part.

I ask that throughout my life You would, by Your Holy Spirit, enlighten me whenever I begin to rely on my own strength and efforts to live righteously before You. I ask that in my times of need You would grant me the understanding always to turn to the graces that are in the fullness of Christ to overcome the sins and weaknesses in my life. I declare that I trust in Your grace alone to walk with Christ.

Thank You for the grace You have granted me. Thank You for the grace that has called me into Jesus, forgiven me of every sin, justified me by His work, made me alive by His Spirit and raised me up with Him to sit in heavenly places. Thank You for Your grace, which is always sufficient for all my needs for all of my life.

Now, Father, help me as I go forward in Your grace, serving You, representing You and touching the lives of others with the power of Your grace.

In Jesus' name, Amen.

Subject Index

Isaac, 70, 71, 72
Isaiah, 111, 124, 163
Ishmael, 70, 71, 72
Islam, 15
Israel, 55–56, 58–59, 75, 122, 155

James, 85–86, 170
Jeremiah, 74
Jesus Christ, 88
  death of, 26, 40, 47, 64–65,
    127–37, 187
  dependence on, 74
  disciples of, 90–91
  earthly ministry of, 123–24, 215
  on law, 34–35, 36–38, 53–54
  receiving, 176–77
  relationship with, 8, 150
  second coming of, 202
  sufficiency of, 182–84
  as the way, 162
jewelry, 17
John, 86–89, 92, 176–77
Jordan River, 212–13
Joshua, 106, 145
journey, 61, 95, 96, 97
joy, 59
Judaism, 42, 55–56, 68–69, 76
Judas Iscariot, 89
judgment, 41–42, 108, 118, 166
justice, 163–66, 173
justification, 67, 75

Ketuvim, 53
King's College, 146
knowledge, 50, 76, 99, 101–3, 108,
  109

language, 147–48
law
  civil, 12–13
  effects of, 57–77
  as means of righteousness, 129–
    31, 157
  of Moses, 14–15, 31, 33–46
  purpose of, 47–56
  requirement of, 80–85

vs. grace, 9, 11–12, 20–21, 61–62,
  139–40
  work of, 16
legalism, 7, 45, 46, 66–67, 71–72,
  147, 157–58
Levitical blessing, 121, 195–96
liberty, 9, 64, 66, 85–86
life, 125–26, 144, 199, 212–13
light, 101–3, 185, 199
love, 98, 115
  meaning of, 89
  as obedience, 90–93
  outpouring of, 103–5
  as requirement, 82–86
lust, 178
lying, 15–16

Magnificat, 171–72
makeup, 17
marriage, 42–43, 114–15
martyrdom, 24, 28
Mary, 171–72
maturity, 100, 105
meat, 17, 18
mediator, 150
mercy, 118, 164–66, 173
Messiah, 205
Methodists, 40, 72
miracles, 28, 99, 215
Moses, 20–21, 33–37, 70, 121,
  144–46, 150, 154–55
motivation, 71, 73–74, 77, 85–86,
  211
movies, 17, 18, 157
multiplication, 105
murderers, 23–24, 28–30, 74, 85

Naomi, 89
Nevi'im, 53
new birth, 177, 184
New Covenant, 106, 140–52
Noah, 120, 196

obedience, 54, 90–93
offerings, 22–23, 151
Old Testament, 53, 142–52
openness, 97
Orpah, 89

224

speech, 148, 207, 211
Spirit-filled life, 61, 64, 80
stewardship, 216
sufficiency, 182–84, 213–16
supernatural testimony, 27–28

Talmud, 37
Tarsus, 60
temptation, 73, 76, 179, 203
Ten Commandments, 14, 41, 129
thankfulness, 205–8
theologians, 81
theology, 133–34
timidity, 178
Titus, 200
Torah, 37, 53
transformation, 65, 176
transgression, 62–63
truth, 20, 96

victory, 60, 110, 132, 198
virtue, 108

"wall of separation," 39–42
war, 86
weakness, 182–83, 214–15
wealth, 76, 209
Wesley, Charles, 127
Wesley, John, 71–72
wisdom, 101, 190, 214
works, 25, 26, 29, 36, 153–67,
174–75, 181
worry, 178–79
wrath, 62–63, 118
writings, 37, 53

youth camps, 17

Scripture Index

Genesis

1:1 87
3:5 76
3:17 25
4:1–5 22
4:1–8 24
4:4 24
4:5 24
4:6–8 23
6:8 120, 196
15:5–6 159
15:6 112, 159

Exodus

2:23–25 122
34:29–35 146

Leviticus

24:17–20 165

Numbers

4:20 129
6:22–26 121
6:24–26 195
23:9 55

Deuteronomy

4:2 34, 155
12:32 155
12:32 34
27:26 155

1 Samuel

6:19 129

Psalms

5:12 199
14:2–3 126
32:1–2 160
45:2 205
59:17 165
112 211
112:9 211

Proverbs

4:23 149
11:24–25 213
16:15 199
23:23 101
27:6 89

Isaiah

9:1–2 123–24
28:17 163
45:21 163
53:10 135
61:10 112

Jeremiah

17:6 66
31:31–34 148–49

Habakkuk

2:4 75

Matthew

3:10 77
4:12–16 123–24
5:17 36
5:17–18 34–35
9:12–13 49
10:7–8 211–12
22:35 81
22:35–36 81
22:35–40 81
22:37–40 82

Luke

John

Acts

Romans

1 Corinthians

2 Corinthians

Galatians

229

ABOUT
the
AUTHOR

Derek Prince (1915–2003) was born in India of British parents. Educated as a scholar of Greek and Latin at Eton College and Cambridge University, England, he held a Fellowship in Ancient and Modern Philosophy at King's College. He also studied several modern languages, including Hebrew and Aramaic, at Cambridge University and the Hebrew University in Jerusalem.

While serving with the British army in World War II, he began to study the Bible and experienced a life-changing encounter with Jesus Christ. Out of this encounter he formed two conclusions: first, that Jesus Christ is alive; second, that the Bible is a true, relevant, up-to-date book. These conclusions altered the whole course of his life, which he then devoted to studying and teaching the Bible.

Derek's main gift of explaining the Bible and its teaching in a clear and simple way has helped build a foundation of faith in millions of lives. His non-denominational, non-sectarian approach has made his teaching equally relevant and helpful to people from all racial and religious backgrounds.

He is the author of over 50 books, 600 audio and 100 video teachings, many of which have been translated and published in more than 100 languages. His daily radio broadcast is translated into Arabic, Chinese (Amoy, Cantonese, Mandarin, Shanghaiese, Swatow), Croatian, German, Malagasy, Mongolian, Russian, Samoan, Spanish and Tongan. The radio program continues to touch lives around the world.

Derek Prince Ministries persists in reaching out to believers in over 140 countries with Derek's teachings, fulfilling the mandate to keep on "until Jesus returns." This is effected through the outreaches of more than 45 Derek Prince offices around the world, including primary work in Australia, Canada, China, France, Germany, the Netherlands, New Zealand, Norway, Russia, South Africa, Switzerland, the United Kingdom and the United States. For current information about these and other worldwide locations, visit www.derekprince.com.

Books by Derek Prince

Appointment in Jerusalem
At the End of Time *
Authority and Power of God's Word *
Be Perfect
Blessing or Curse: You Can Choose
Bought With Blood
By Grace Alone
Called to Conquer
Choice of a Partner, The
Complete Salvation
Declaring God's Word
Derek Prince—A Biography by
    Stephen Mansfield
Derek Prince: On Experiencing
    God's Power
Destiny Of Israel and The Church,
Divine Exchange, The
Doctrine of Baptisms, The *
Does Your Tongue Need Healing?
End of Life's Journey, The
Entering the Presence of God
Expelling Demons
Explaining Blessings and Curses
Extravagant Love
Faith and Works *
Faith to Live By
Fasting
Final Judgment *
First Mile, The
Foundational Truths For Christian
    Living
Founded On the Rock *
Gateway to God's Blessing
Gifts of the Spirit, The
God Is a Matchmaker
God's Medicine Bottle
God's Plan for Your Money
God's Remedy for Rejection
God's Will for Your Life
God's Word Heals
Grace of Yielding, The
Harvest Just Ahead, The
Holy Spirit in You, The
How to Fast Successfully
Husbands and Fathers

I Forgive You
Immersion in The Spirit *
Judging
Laying the Foundations Series
Life's Bitter Pool
Living As Salt and Light
Lucifer Exposed
Marriage Covenant, The
Orphans, Widows, the Poor and
    Oppressed
Our Debt to Israel
Pages from My Life's Book
Partners for Life
Philosophy, the Bible and the
    Supernatural
Power in the Name
Power of the Sacrifice, The
Prayers and Proclamations
Praying for the Government
Protection from Deception
Promise of Provision, The
Promised Land
Prophetic Guide to the End Times
Receiving God's Best
Rediscovering God's Church
Resurrection of the Body *
Rules of Engagement
Secrets of a Prayer Warrior
Self-Study Bible Course (revised and
expanded)
Set Apart For God
Shaping History Through Prayer
    and Fasting
Spiritual Warfare
Surviving the Last Days
They Shall Expel Demons
Through Repentance to Faith *
Through the Psalms with
    Derek Prince
Transmitting God's Power *
War in Heaven
Who Is the Holy Spirit?
You Matter to God
You Shall Receive Power

*Foundations Series

1. Founded on the Rock (B100)
2. Authority and Power of God's Word (B101)
3. Through Repentance to Faith (B102)
4. Faith and Works (B103)
5. The Doctrine of Baptisms (B104)
6. Immersion in The Spirit (B105)
7. Transmitting God's Power (B106)
8. At the End of Time (B107)
9. Resurrection of the Body (B108)
10. Final Judgment (B109)

www.derekprince.com

DEREK PRINCE MINISTRIES
OFFICES WORLDWIDE

ASIA/ PACIFIC
DPM–Asia/Pacific
38 Hawdon Street, Sydenham,
Christchurch 8023,
New Zealand
T: + 64 3 366 4443
E: admin@dpm.co.nz
W: www.dpm.co.nz and
www.derekprince.in

AUSTRALIA
DPM–Australia
Unit 21, 317-321, Woodpark Road,
Smithfield, New South Wales 2146,
Australia
T: +61-2-9604-0670
E: enquiries@derekprince.com.au
W: www.derekprince.com.au

CANADA
DPM–Canada
P. O. Box 8354 Halifax,
Nova Scotia B3K 5M1, Canada
T: + 1 902 443 9577
E: enquiries.dpm@eastlink.ca
W: www.derekprince.org

FRANCE
DPM–France
B.P. 31, Route d'Oupia,
34210 Olonzac, France
T: + 33 468 913872
E: info@derekprince.fr
W: www.derekprince.fr

GERMANY
DPM–Germany
Schwarzauer Str. 56,
D-83308 Trostberg, Germany
T: + 49 8621 64146
E: IBL.de@t-online.de
W: www.ibl-dpm.net

NETHERLANDS
DPM–Netherlands
Postbus 326,
7100 AH Winterswijk,
The Netherlands
T: +31 (0) 251 255 044
E: info@dpmnederland.nl
W: www.dpmnederland.nl

NORWAY
P. O. Box 129 Lodderfjord,
N-5881, Bergen,
Norway
T: +47 928 39855
E: sverre@derekprince.no
W: www.derekprince.no

SINGAPORE
Derek Prince Publications Pte. Ltd.
P. O. Box 2046,
Robinson Road Post Office,
Singapore 904046
T: + 65 6392 1812
E: dpmchina@singnet.com.sg
English web: www.dpmchina.org
Chinese web: www.ygmweb.org

SOUTH AFRICA
DPM–South Africa
P. O. Box 33367,
Glenstantia 0010 Pretoria,
South Africa
T: +27 12 348 9537
E: enquiries@derekprince.co.za
W: www.derekprince.co.za

SWITZERLAND
DPM–Switzerland
Alpenblick 8,
CH-8934 Knonau,
Switzerland
T: + 41(0) 44 768 25 06
E: dpm-ch@ibl-dpm.net
W: www.ibl-dpm.net

UNITED KINGDOM
DPM–UK
Kingsfield, Hadrian Way,
Baldock SG7 6AN, UK
T: + 44 (0) 1462 492100
E: enquiries@dpmuk.org
W: www.dpmuk.org

USA
DPM–USA
P. O. Box 19501,
Charlotte NC 28219, USA
T: + 1 704 357 3556
E: ContactUs@derekprince.org
W: www.derekprince.org

Lightning Source UK Ltd.
Milton Keynes UK
UKOW041100020713

9 781908 594